The Gift of Attitude ©

The Most Inspiring Ways to Create
Exceptional Experiences for Others

Sam Glenn
The Attitude Guy ©

Published 2012, 2014
ISBN 978-1-63068-745-8

To my wife, who demonstrates every day

the true meaning of the gift of attitude.

It's the gift that keeps on giving

> *People will forget what you said, people will forget what you did, but people will never forget how you made them feel.*
>
> **– Maya Angelou**

Table of Contents

Sam Glenn

The Gift of Attitude is...

(Just in) A commercial airplane with Frontier Airlines was extremely delayed and had been rerouted to another airport due to bad weather. They had been waiting for hours for the storms to clear up so they could take off and reach their final destination. The pilot recognized that the passengers were getting tense and feeling frustrated from sitting so long. (I've been in that situation and personally speaking, watching paint dry is more exciting.) The time was almost 10 p.m. when the pilot, *Gerhard Brandner*, made a choice. He decided to let everyone on the plane know that he was thinking of them and had their best interests at heart. He was about to create an exceptional experience that nobody would soon forget. But I don't think he was doing it for the recognition or publicity. He was just doing what he felt was the right thing in the moment and doing what he would want someone to do for him. He ordered Domino's Pizza for the entire plane (136 passengers) and paid for it out of his own pocket. It was his way of sharing a little attitude – *helping others make the best of an unexpected setback.*

This story made national headlines because it was so out of the ordinary that it had to be shared. We have all been in those moments that have us shaking our head in frustration, but what an awesome example of how a little attitude can turn things around– that and some cheesy pizza! Let me ask this, did the pilot have to order pizza for everyone? No he did not. Did he make his airline look like the best airline in the world that day? Yes, even in the midst of frustrating setbacks. Did his actions improve the attitude of the passengers? Oh yeah it did. He made everyone feel like they had not been forgotten or just another number doing business with a large company! And finally, did the pilot create a memorable and magical story that spread like a wild fire? Well, I just told you about it and millions of others have heard about it and read about it in the news. So what was that one thing that made such a big difference? You are about to find out exactly what it is and a whole lot more in the following pages. I am excited to share with you some of the very best ways to create the most exceptional experiences for others and all with the magical touch of your attitude.

It's a fact, we give it away every day to our family, friends, co-workers, customers and strangers—our attitude. The gift of attitude is simple, yet so potent in all the unique and special ways it can make a positive difference. It's a difference maker for us when we choose the right attitude that works for us; it's a difference maker for others when we choose an attitude that comes from the heart. The gift of attitude is simply choosing an attitude that makes a positive impact in your life and in the lives of other people. This book is about developing your attitude sense. It's about recognizing, utilizing and building more strength into your attitude. It's being aware of and working on the weak points in your attitude. And finally, it's about being open to implementing new ideas on how to use your attitude to create experiences that make others feel important, valued and cared for. Your attitude is a story maker and I am excited to share with you some of my own personal stories that highlight the gift of attitude. There is no limit to with whom or where you can give the treasured gift of attitude. It is what people know you for and will ultimately remember you by. It will be your legacy.

A friend sent me the following story and, after I read it, I thought it summed up the simplicity of how we can use our attitude as a special gift.

During my second month of nursing school, our

professor gave us a pop quiz. I had breezed through the questions, until I read the last one: "What is the first name of the woman who cleans the school?"

Surely, this was some kind of joke. I had seen the cleaning woman several times. She was tall, dark-haired, and in her 50s; but how would I know her name? I handed in my paper, leaving the last question blank.

Just before class ended, one student asked if the last question would count toward our quiz grade.

"Absolutely," said the professor. "In your careers, you will meet many people. All are significant. They deserve your attention and care, even if all you do is smile and say 'hello.'"

I've never forgotten that lesson.

I also learned her name was Dorothy.

Just acknowledging someone with a smile or simple greeting is a gift of attitude. I love that story because it highlights that the simplest things can make others feel important and recognized. We all have the ability to do this.

Sam Glenn

The Gift of a
Positive Attitude

I admit, I don't remember her name, but I will never forget her attitude and what a gift her attitude was to me. Years ago, I met a local business owner who I only knew as *'the vitamin store lady'*. She had told me her name (perhaps a few times), but I forgot it. I will admit that I am one of those people who struggle with remembering people's names. I have tried to get better and more proficient with names; however, the vitamin store lady was skillful at remembering me every time I walked into her shop, "Well hello there, Mr. Sam Glenn! You look an inch taller!"

Once a month I would stop by her vitamin and

13

nutrition store to grab a box of protein bars, extra strength fiber and a bottle of Fred Flintstone chewable vitamins. It was a small list of items, but all things I needed—perhaps some of which I just shared too much with you.

When I first met the vitamin store lady and encountered her positivity, I wasn't sure if it was real or whether she just had eaten way too many happy vitamins. But with each visit to her store, I discovered she was the real deal. She walked the talk and her attitude led the way. I got to know her a little better with each visit. She reminded me of a loving grandma who enjoys looking out for her grandkids. I think her best marketing strategy for business development was her attitude. I was so impressed with the service, kindness and personability that I told everyone I knew to go there. She didn't ask me to spread the word and I didn't get anything in return or kickbacks on sales for referring people to go there. I was simply a happy customer and happy customers like to spread the good word. The reason I told everyone is when you have an experience that makes your day, you want others, people you care for, to have that similar experience. I knew anyone I told would be treated right and as an added bonus - leave the vitamin store feeling good about themselves and life.

When I left the vitamin lady's store, I always felt a little pep in my step or like my attitude got a surge of positive energy. She just had that way of being so encouraging, making you smile and making you feel good about life.

Doing what I do, speaking to organizations about the gift of attitude as it relates to achieving success in life and at work, I began to pay closer attention to the vitamin store lady. I wanted to make sure her attitude wasn't just for show. I wanted to find out her motivation for treating people so well. She stood out from the crowd when it comes to creating positive experiences for others. If I had to rate her attitude, I would put it in the rock star attitude hall a fame! I might speak and write on the subject of attitude for a living, but the learning never ends. This was a classroom opportunity for me and I was going to seize it.

On one of my routine visits to her shop, I thought it would be nice to give her as a gift some copies of my latest book, *A Kick in the Attitude*. She was so thrilled that you thought her name just got announced on the Price is Right; *"COME ON DOWN! You're the next contestant on the Price is Right!"*

We engaged in a conversation about attitude for nearly an hour. I mostly listened. This was her time to shine and she dazzled my mind with her remarkable stories. She shared about her family and all the rough times they had gone through and how they survived and became closer. She talked about why she started her business and how growing a new business can be challenging on a limited budget.

Everything she communicated somehow found a tie back to having the right attitude. And as if her attitude wasn't enough, she had this infectious laugh that didn't quite sound normal, but it was hilarious. It was the kind of laugh you hear and it makes you start laughing. Do you know someone with that laugh? Is it you? I love that laugh!

Before I left her store, she had me sign the books I gave her and reached up to give me a monster momma bear hug. And as I was walking out the door, a friend I told about the vitamin shop was walking in. How cool was that?

As I walked to my car with the biggest smile on my face, I felt recharged. I thought, *"Wow that made my day! I feel like Tony the Tiger. I feel great and it didn't even involve Frosted Flakes. When I give my speeches, I want others to know this feeling and experience."*

The holidays had snuck up on me and most of the yellow and red leafs had fallen to the ground. I enjoy all the seasons of the year, but the Fall in the Midwest has to be my favorite time of the year. My speaking schedule was pretty hectic and I was traveling all over the country. I was feeling pretty exhausted and started to feel the symptoms of a cold coming on. All the travel I was doing, it was wearing me down a little. It was time to load up on some vitamin C.

On this particular day, I had to be at the airport by 2:30pm to catch a flight to Texas, so my plan was to leave the house a little early and pop into the vitamin shop to get some vitamin C. By this time, whenever I went to the vitamin store, I was smiling before I even walked in the door. I knew the vitamin store lady would be there to help me feel better with some vitamins and her attitude.

The bell rang as I walked through the store door and, as I was trying to stomp off some of the snow on the placemat, something didn't seem the same. When I looked up from making sure the snow was off my shoes, I saw a white haired elderly man working behind the counter. I had never seen him before. Was he new? I scanned the entire store really fast and the vitamin store lady wasn't there. It must have been her day off or maybe she ran out for lunch. I grabbed a bottle of vitamin C and placed it on the counter to pay.

"How's your day going?" I said with a smile to

the man working the counter.

He only nodded and didn't look at me, "It's fine, I suppose."

The white haired man working behind the counter seemed lost, dazed and relatively out of it, plus his short responses seemed cold. I thought to myself, *If the vitamin store lady knew this guy was so gloomy serving customers, she would not be pleased.*

So, I inquired of him if the owner would be back anytime soon. The man's head just dropped, and it was all he could do to hold it together. Now I was confused. I asked, "Are you okay, man? Do you need something?"

He slowly lifted his head and instantly I could see pain in his eyes as they swelled with tears and he summoned what looked to be part of a smile, but not quite. And with a soft gentle tone in his voice that was barely above a whisper, he asked, "Are you by chance the motivational speaker guy?"

"Uhhh... Yes, I am."

"I recognize you from the picture on your book.

My wife, who owns this shop, talked about you all the time. She shared your book with me also."

"Ohh, so you're her husband—it is so good to finally meet you! Your wife mentioned you in a few of her stories ... but all good stuff though."

He half smiled and said, "Yeah ... she has some good stories and we will sure miss her."

"Huhh??? What happened?!!!"

And then he shared, "My wife started to get sick a few weeks ago, and we found out she had advanced leukemia. We started treatment, but it was too late. She passed away four days ago. I am here trying to keep her store running. She always looked forward to when you would stop in. She talked about your book and that you would make her day by making her laugh."

My stomach just dropped. I got that sick feeling and look of pure shock. I stayed for as long as I could to offer some comfort and support. Before I left the shop, I told him, "Your wife was always so nice to me, and had such an amazing attitude. She always made my day and her attitude was such a gift."

He let out a little breath and mustered a look of remembrance as if he could see his wife right in front of him, "Yes sir, she was a gift to us all."

I feel bad that I don't remember her name, but I know one thing for sure—I will never forget her attitude. She used her attitude to grow her business. She used it to get through rough times with her family. She used it to be a great wife and to raise her kids. She used it to make a customer's day. She used it to be a friend. She used it up until the end, but the legacy of her attitude will live on. That, my friend, is an example of what it means to use your attitude as a gift.

Sam Glenn

Our Attitude is Either in the Way or Making a Way

I was waiting in the service line at Meijer. They had multiple people helping customers who were returning items. Since they ship postal packages there and the post office was on the other side of town, I thought I would pop in really fast and ship a few book orders.

"Next... Can I help you sir?"

"Yes, I would like to mail out a few packages priority mail please."

"Okay.....Uhhhh ... sir, I think someone is trying to get your attention."

I looked over my left shoulder and observed a woman giving me some major stink eye—that unpleasant glare someone gives you when they are not happy with you. She was glaring at me like I just stole her puppy or borrowed her car, returned it on empty and left crouton crumbs all over the seat. I was immediately confused, because I wasn't aware that I did anything to deserve the stink eye, so I inquired, "Yes, can I help you?"

With a scowling look and a huff of breath, "Yeah ... you're in my way! Move your big butt, Bigfoot! I can't move! You need to move!"

My eyes doubled in size as I was in a little taken back by the words she just threw at me like an unexpected snowball to the face. I did a quick scan of the area behind where I was standing and it was apparent that were was a good five feet of extra room between me and the other customers waiting in line. I started to mildly laugh because it seemed so out of the ordinary that someone would speak that way to anyone like that. And how much actual room there was to move past me. She could have pushed two or three full carts past me. For a split second, I didn't know if she joking and recognized me from my speeches. Sometimes people will joke with me in public to see if I walk my talk, so I thought this was one of those moments. But, after a few more elapsed seconds, it was clear she was dead serious about her request (command) for me to relocate my Bigfoot big butt.

She was pushing a cart that was overflowing with groceries and for some very unusual and outrageous reason didn't think there was enough room to move past me. So, to rectify the situation, I gracefully apologized to her and made my best attempt to squeeze closer toward the service counter—so she would have enough room to move past me.

However, the vibe I got from this lady told me that she was in an awfully bad mood, feeling miserable and had a craving to share those negative sentiments with others. I just happened to be in the path the tornado. Or her tornado like attitude. That's the thing about people who are gloom and doom—they want others to be miserable too. She could have said three simple words that would've prevented her off Broadway production of *Negativity and Drama*, *"Excuse me, please."*

I mean, don't we get farther in life with a little sugar and honey? She was trying to get her way with rotten eggs and bad apples.

(*On a side note to this story*: For the sake of this book and keeping it in the light of positivity, I changed the actual words that this incredibly cranky lady used to ask me to move. She did call me Bigfoot and made reference to me having an immense backside, but she seasoned those words with some other not so pleasant words – toxic and negative words. Let's just say, when I was six years old, I tried using some of the same words at a church function and it didn't go over so well. My parents and other guests were in such shock; I remember hearing someone suggest dipping me into Holy Water or performing an exorcism. I was just a kid who heard some words and tried to incorporate them into my vocabulary. I learned that some words are just better left out of our everyday vocabulary. My very embarrassed mom washed my mouth out with soap and made it clear that if I used words like that again I would be paying a special visit to Jesus. I got in even more trouble for back talking when I responded, *"I wanna meet Jesus! I heard he is nice to children and doesn't force them to eat soap and vegetables and lets them have candy and choose their own bedtime."*)

The woman who just verbally belittled me in public had an odd look to her. And trust me, you know the look. I call it the look of choice. Every day we get to choose our own attitude and how we will use it in life and at work. When you choose an attitude that is unpleasant, it displays a look on your face that might have people wondering if you need extra fiber in your diet. It's a grumpy, uptight, sour, testy, sullen look that gives the impression you may be wearing underwear that is way too tight. Are you getting the picture? *(Are you possibly thinking of someone in particular right now, hmmmmm?)*

As the cranky lady rolled her cart past me she wanted to leave one final impression. She huffed at me. It was the sound I imagine the real Bigfoot might make. It was an actual huff of breath to let me know one last time that she was not my number one fan. Even though I did nothing wrong, said nothing wrong and had no intention of doing anything wrong, I just happened to be in the path of her negative attitude. I turned back to the kid helping me at the service desk and we both had a similar look—our eyes were practically bugging out by what we just witnessed. The other customers, waiting in line, were shaking their heads in disapproval by what they just observed in the epic battle of positive versus negative.

Let me ask you this, have you ever encountered someone like this cranky lady? Did it put a hiccup in your day? Did you think, stubbing my toe would be a joy compared to having to deal with this person?

Maybe you thought, "*Why do people have to act like that? Why are they so negative and feel inclined and entitled to make others feel the same?*"

It's frustrating, I know. And if you don't address it the right way, it can eat you up and turn your turn your attitude rotten like bananas that sat out too long.

Sam Glenn

Exterminate
Attitude Termites

The cranky woman who just told me I have a big butt and called me Bigfoot was gone from the scene, but her negative impact was still there, resonating with everyone. A woman who had been standing in line waiting walked up to me and quietly said, with a gentle smile, *"It's ok young man, some people just wear their underpants too tight. That woman didn't need to act that way towards you. Don't let it eat you up. You handled it perfectly."*

Moments like that make me smile. She was what I call an attitude warrior. Attitude warriors swoop in

31

and lift each other up when someone tries to knock us down with their negativity. She was giving me a piece of her attitude to counter the negative effects of the cranky lady's attitude.

I have a little philosophy that goes like this, *"Your attitude is either in the way or making a way and you determine which every day."*

When you choose the right attitude, it becomes a gift to yourself. When you choose the right attitude and give it away, it becomes a gift to others. When you use your attitude the right way, it becomes one of your greatest assets. When we choose the right attitude, it becomes an unstoppable force that partners with our efforts to achieve our goals. The right attitude opens new doors and seeks out the best solutions when faced with setbacks. Our attitude is always at work—working for us or against us. Our attitude works diligently through our abilities, education and experiences. Every day, we get to choose the face of our attitude— to be positive or to be average and negative. Our attitude is a communicator.

It communicates who we are and what we are about. The same is true for whatever organization you work for—your attitude drives culture. Are people lining up outside your door or turning away and going on to the next one?

Unfortunately, a positive attitude doesn't stop tough times from knocking at your door, but it does give you is the mental muscle to deal with difficulties more effectively than a negative attitude can. When you choose the right attitude, it becomes a gift you give to yourself; when you share the right attitude with others, it becomes a generous gift to them. Every day and in every way we are giving our attitude away to others.

So the questions I have for you are these:

- *Do others recognize your attitude as a gift or a nightmare?*
- *Is your attitude working for you or against you?*
- *Does your attitude make people happy*

that they work with you, know you, bumped into you or do business with you?

- *Which takes up more space in your attitude – Drama and Negativity or Positivity and Optimism?*
- *Do you use your attitude in way that makes a difference?*

The sign of a true and genuine attitude warrior is someone who places an incredible amount of emphasis, priority and substantial worth on having a positive attitude. They know for a fact – "A FACT" – that their attitude is relevant to everything in their personal life and work life. They understand their attitude plays the lead role in everything and if it is not working for them, then it is costing them.

(Think about your attitude for just a moment and how it communicates to others on a daily basis – family, co-workers, strangers you may encounter at the service desk, in traffic, customers – and to yourself! Are you using your attitude as a gift? Are you choosing an attitude that is a gift to yourself? Taking a fast moment to reflect on this will enhance your attitude awareness. It will give you a greater sense how you are using your attitude.)

A Classic
Attitude Showdown

I finished paying to ship out my book orders at the service desk, turned and made my way to the exit. I knew that I shouldn't let how the cranky lady treated me get to me. One of my biggest pet peeves are people who are rude and display the least amount of care and courtesy towards others. That unhelpful attitude is reflected in the level of work they do in the workplace. Believe me, it's quite evident. They are what you might call clock punchers. They show up to work, punch the time clock and automatically put the mental cruise control on until they clock out.

They may show up physically, but everything else is on vacation or sitting on the couch at home eating chips. We don't always get a glimpse of internal issues that might happen in the workplace that reflect mediocre behavior, but as customers we hear and witness disheartening stories every day in our service experiences. Have you ever been treated so poorly that you wonder how the company is still in business? *"Is that how you treat a paying customer? A loyal customer? A repeat customer? A customer with cash?"*

Sometimes it seems that, when we are treated poorly, we let it eat us up. We can't stop thinking about it and it becomes a negative distraction. I call that getting infected with attitude termites. That is what attitude termites do, they get into our mind and just eat away at our positive perspective until we start to think the wrong way. I started thinking of things I could have said back to her at the service desk or what I would say if I saw her again. I wanted to buy her fiber as a special gift. Instead of focusing on the rest of my day and the plans I had, I was stressing and replaying a past negative experience. I was letting the cranky lady win the battle for my attitude. This is why it is so important to work on feeding your attitude positive stuff every day, so it becomes immune to attitude termites. I will share some ideas on that in the following pages.

The thing about attitude – and I will say it over and over – is that our attitude is our choice. You choose your attitude in how you do your work, treat others and respond to situations. The late Jim Rohn said it best, *"Don't spend your time trying to get even with others, but rather choose to get ahead."*

Oftentimes, if we dwell long enough on negative things people do and say, it builds up the desire to want to give them a taste of their own treatment. That is called getting even. Attitude warriors are about getting ahead. Life will present you with enough opportunities to choose to get even or get ahead. When I walked out the exit doors of Meijer, I was about to be presented with that opportunity.

Sam Glenn

The Way of
an Attitude Warrior

The exit doors to the store opened and, once I stepped out into the sunny cool day, I took a deep breath and let go of what just happened inside. I started walking towards my truck, raised my phone to see what time it was and then glanced forward to remotely unlock my doors. But, to my surprise I saw the cranky lady in front of me, about 20 yards away, on the ground and struggling to get up. She looked hurt. This was the woman who just informed me and half the store that I had genetic ties to Bigfoot. I had a choice, do I get even and blurt out, *"Hey you crazy cranky lady -that's what you get for being so mean!*

And if I look like Bigfoot, it's because I haven't shaved in four days...or effectively applied ample deodorant to certain regions of my human body!"

Or do I get ahead by demonstrating the way of an attitude warrior? There was a time in my life when I had a very low appraisal for attitude and would have easily been reactive and said some things to get even. But, now my attitude is my greatest asset, my super power for making a difference, my most relevant tool for facing negativity and my closest companion in the pursuit of my ambitions. My attitude was now working by choice, rather by random chance. Nobody other than me can choose my attitude and how I will apply it to life. That is my ownership as it is yours.

She was on the ground and looked hurt. At first I thought she may have got into a physical altercation with someone in the parking lot and lost the fight. But, nobody was around and I didn't see any cars screeching their tires to hightail it out of there. There, laying on the ground, holding her leg in pain, was the cranky lady who had just embarrassed me, talked down to me, was rude, negative and told me my butt was oversized. Some might chalk this up to karma, but I saw it as something else. While I do believe that karma is very real and has its place in life, this wasn't one of those moments. This was an opportunity for me to be an attitude warrior and plant the example of what the right attitude is all about. She tried to give me some of her attitude and it didn't work. I sent her attitude termites scrambling. This was an open door for me to give her the gift of my attitude.

I rushed over to her, "Are you okay?"

Painfully, she responded, "I lost my balance and fell on my knee."

"Okay, are you able to stand up at all?"

"I think so…"

"Grab my arm with both hands and I will lift you up."

And, just like that, my Bigfoot big butt lifted her up off the ground. I felt more like Superman in the moment. She bent over to rub her knee and brush off the dirt. I remember thinking it's a good thing she was wearing jeans or her knee would have been shredded up from the concrete parking lot. She slowly limped next to me as I voluntarily pushed her cart to her car and assisted by loading everything into the trunk. I asked again if she was okay and she nodded with a painful expression, grabbed my hand and patted it a few times in a gesture of appreciation and softly said, *"Thank you, sir."*

She gave me the one motion wave as she slowly drove out of the store parking lot and I nodded back to her with a half-smile—almost like a superhero would do in the movies. It felt good to do the right thing. Even though she didn't apologize for calling me unnecessary Neanderthal names in the store, I was content with the outcome. I would like to think that maybe I did something for her that maybe restored a little hope in humanity and made her think that not all people are bad. I don't know her story, but who knows, maybe the attitude termites ate up all her positive perspectives and she just became comfortable with being cranky and that is how she lived every day. It was evident that her attitude was not working for her. And so I stepped up and I gave her some of mine. That is what it means to give others the gift of your attitude. I am an attitude warrior and so my attitude is my greatest strength and super power. I choose to use it in ways that everyone wins.

Sometimes, to impact our world, our culture, our workplace and life, we just need a little infusion of positivity to clear away some of the negative fog that prevents us from thinking clearly. That boost of positivity will assist us to think in such a way that we make choices that reward us instead of leading us to the garbage dump of regret. A little positivity can permeate into our interactions with others and be one of the most incredible gifts someone can receive. When you give someone the gift of attitude, it infuses their life with renewed energy, a memorable story to remember and live by. Attitude warriors understand that sometimes our attitude can become drained of its strength and that we need to take the time to recharge. We cannot live at our best and reach new peaks operating on empty, so you have to ask yourself this, "What is the consequence of not taking the time to recharge my attitude? What is the consequence of not taking the time at work to recharge attitudes?" Once you answer those questions, honestly, you will begin to see greater value in your attitude. You will begin to hold it up to the light like a fine diamond. Instead of letting it run on zero and begin collecting dust, you will start to make it a bigger priority.

An attitude warrior also recognizes that, when someone's attitude isn't working for them or others in a favorable way, sharing a little bit of theirs can make all the difference in the world.

That is the gift of attitude!

What Was Once Worth Pennies, Is Now Priceless

I can relate to the cranky lady and the reason I can relate so well is I used to have an attitude similar to hers. My attitude was in the way and working against me and what I wanted in life. I didn't place a high value on my attitude. It's a word that is so overused and misused that it didn't seem relevant to me. There was a time when if you'd asked me to appraise my attitude I would have said it is worth pennies. But, I am no longer the same person. I don't think the same way now.

As the saying goes, *"I once was blind, and now I see."*

If you have read any of my other books or know my background story, you will know that I wasn't always the most positive person in the world. I didn't buy into this attitude stuff.

Consequently, I became an expert on negativity and learned quickly that a negative attitude doesn't get you hired, promoted or attract the right people into your life. I was sleeping on my mom's living room floor, working nights as a janitor and letting the attitude termites eat up any ambition or dreams I might have had for myself. I was depressed, defeated and filled with doubt. I had taken ownership of my grandfather's business and due to some unfortunate circumstances lost it all. I was broke, in debt and homeless. My mom was generous enough to let me stay with her in her apartment until I was able to get back on my feet. My bed was the living room floor for over 2 years.

A good friend took me out for some coffee, that I could not even afford, and we began to talk about how my attitude had become the root of most of my problems. With his encouragement, I started to make a concentrated effort to fix my broken attitude. As I did, my life changed. How I handled adversity changed. How I treated others changed. I wasn't always trying to think negatively. As I explored this attitude stuff a little more wholeheartedly, I learned that this attitude stuff is really a big deal. It saddens me when people miss how relevant attitude is to the work they do and the life they live. When giving speeches, I like to tell my audiences that I didn't choose the subject of attitude. It chose me. I was already an expert on being negative and what I learned being in that place was valuable to my journey ahead.

For years, the whole concept of my attitude and the role it played in my life and work wasn't front and center in my mind. I didn't think much about it. I went off the little information I knew about attitude.

Growing up we all hear are talks, speeches and lectures that tie back into our attitude and how we need to change our attitude, or have the right attitude. But, for myself, I never really understood it. I just went with the flow. My attitude was vulnerable to the roll of the dice and took on the form of whatever my circumstances were. So when things were bad, my attitude would get bad. When things were good, my attitude was fine. It became whatever was going on. I didn't use it to overcome setbacks, make a difference or achieve my ambitions. I just went with the flow.

However, I do remember a small breakthrough that helped me gain a greater appraisal for attitude. It was when the doctor told my mom she had breast cancer and that her treatment would be 10% what they do and 90% my mom's attitude. If that doesn't put things into perspective, I don't know what does. Our attitude is more relevant than you could even imagine. The moment you become aware of this, and make your attitude a priority, you will begin to live in such a way that life will never be the same. I am living proof.

I never set out to be an author or motivational speaker. I was too scared to give speeches in school, so I took zeros and F's with enthusiasm. I was afraid of embarrassing myself and got so nervous that my heart would feel like it was going to explode. My hands would get so wet with sweat and the back of my neck would get so tight that it took weeks to get all the knots out.

I didn't like public speaking, so I stopped participating in anything that required it. That all changed when I volunteered to teach Sunday school to high school students. And the saying is true—you do not have to be great to start, but to become great, you gotta start. I was scared, but I had a new attitude and confidence was part of its structure, so I faced my fears and started. I never knew or could have imagined that breaking through my biggest fear would eventually lead to my calling. Beyond our fears is a world of greatness. To get there, we have to be equipped with the right attitude. If you go at your ambitions with the wrong attitude, you will sink the moment pressure and setbacks make their appearance—and they do show up.

For the past 16 years, I have become known as 'The Attitude Guy', and have won multiple awards including Speaker of The Year and Most Outstanding Motivational Video. I credit my success to my attitude partnered with my efforts. The right attitude will either give your efforts strength or weakness. Your attitude is what feeds your efforts.

Now I have the privilege to give nearly 100 speeches a year to organizations and groups who place a substantial value on attitude in the workplace, meaning they value positive people engaged in positive action. It is essential to their culture and the success of their organization. These organizations believe that attitude is like a battery and it gets drained with stress, pressure, deadlines and constant changes. My expertise lies in recharging those attitude batteries so when they go back to work or do business they have the right attitude, feeding positive energy to their efforts. This is a mouthful, but what I do in my speeches for organizations actually leads to greater innovation, creative thinking, gaining an edge over the competition, improved leadership, enhanced communication and teamwork, more sales, upgrading customer experiences and better ways to deal with setbacks. My attitude recharge speeches help people become better people in their personal life. Sometimes the question is complicated but the solution is simple. Sometimes, a simple recharge to the attitude can change everything.

I learn more about attitude every day and it would seem that life is never short of opportunities to put our attitude to the test. But now, instead of seeing attitude as something everyone casually bats around, it has become the cornerstone of my life and work. Attitude is a fascinating subject, and to me more so because the moment I let up even a little bit and stop working on my attitude, I become susceptible to the consequences that come from being attacked by attitude termites—*fear, doubt, laziness, excuses, anger, misery and negativity.*

I absolutely have to work on my attitude every day and make it a priority or I know my relationships will begin to sink; I know my business will dry up; I know I will be burned by the weight of regret. It all starts with attitude. So jumping back a little, when I say I can relate to the cranky lady at the service desk, I get why she was the way she was. I have shaken the hand of negativity enough times to know how it takes over and controls a person's personality and affects how they treat others.

The Gift of Courtesy

Courtesy is a special gift of doing something for someone that they would not expect. The other day, my family was trying out a new BBQ restaurant. We are BBQ fans and if we get a good tip on a new place, we are there. We sat down to our meal and I happened to glance over at the table next to ours and noticed a bowl of baked beans. Now, you can just look at baked beans and tell if they are going to be good or not. Those beans looked so good, I said, "I could roll around in those!" Yeah, I got a few strange looks, mostly from my wife, but I was just trying to express how delicious those beans looked and my desire for wanting them. I excused myself from the table and walked up to the counter to order a side of baked beans. The owner working behind the counter scooped up a big bowl, handed them to me and said, "No charge, hope you enjoy."

I was like, "They are beans, everyone will enjoy them….either now or throughout the day or tonight."

(Some of you may get that attempt at humor later. I grew up with three brothers, so that was our level of humor. I am laughing out loud as I write this. Beans – the musical fruit!! Later, my wife will ask me, "Samuel, what part of your brain thought that was a good idea to put baked bean humor in your book???)

The owner didn't have to give me the beans, but not only did he give me the beans, he also gave me the gift of courtesy. Courtesy is being nice, and doing something for someone that they would not expect. It may be holding a door open, letting someone merge over in traffic or helping someone who is in need in some way.

Another time, after boarding an airplane and grabbing my seat, which was way too small for my human size, my legs were pressed into the seat in front of me and I looked miserable and cramped. It seemed to be a full flight, so I knew there would be no chance of moving or finding a better seat, so I just accepted that I would have to deal with it for a few hours. When everyone had boarded and they went through the safety briefing, a flight attended walked up to me, smiled and said, "Hey, Mr. Long Legs, you want to move? I have a seat up here that may work better for you." *(It's weird - I get called a lot of interesting names being as tall as what I am.)*

I wasn't expecting someone to do that for me at all. That had never happened to me in 16 years of traveling, so for someone to be aware and notice that I was cramped and to go out of their way to find me a new seat was such a gift.

I asked my wife what act of courtesy stands out in mind as her favorite. She said, "Well, it would be nice if people would hold the door as you are going in or out of a building. When you have a big diaper bag and are carrying a baby and car seat, it is always nice when someone waits just a few seconds longer and holds the door. Sadly, most people don't do that and let the door slam into me."

Sometimes there are those moments when we expect people to be courteous and they go out of their way not to be. It can be frustrating. The other day, for instance, I was trying to back out of a parking spot and there was a line of cars behind me and as soon as they moved forward, I could back out. As I slowly backed out, because there was enough room, one car came out of nowhere – really fast – and pulled in right behind me so I could not back out. I hit the brakes hard and was like, "Are you kidding me??!!! That was rude."

I was thinking that it would be kind of cool if we instituted a courtesy law. If people go out of their way to be rude, then they owe you $20, and then, for every act of courtesy, $20 magically appears in your pocket. Could you imagine if that was the case? The shift in how people treat each other and how much more people would go out of their way to be courteous to others. Actually, I kind of think there is a system like this already set up, it's called Karma. Karma is the belief that whatever you send out to others in your attitude and behaviors will come back to you multiplied. Think about that. Do you want your attitude and behaviors coming back to you and multiplying? It does make you think a little, but also gives you a little more awareness.

And there are times that we didn't intend to do something that was discourteous to others. I was driving in downtown Indianapolis and accidently cut someone off driving so I could pull into a McDonald's to grab a coffee. I pulled up to the drive through and I could see in my mirror the person I cut off. They didn't seem too happy. I honestly didn't mean it and when I did it, I said, "Sorry!" but they couldn't hear me saying that in my car. So, when I pulled up to window #2 to pay for my coffee, I gave the drive through cashier an extra $20 and said, "I accidently cut off the guy behind me and want to pay for his meal. If there is any change left over, you can put it in the donation jar for the Ronald McDonald House."

The lady took my $20 and jokingly said, "Wow, I need to have someone like you cut me off every day! That was really nice of you."

I was trying to fix what I did wrong by doing something right. It wasn't much, but when I pulled out of the parking lot I looked back to see how the person whose lunch I'd just paid for responded. First it was a look of confusion, then the cashier pointed at me and when the gentleman in his car looked over, he waved and had the biggest smile ever.

The gift of courtesy is oftentimes a surprise to the heart. Every now and then someone steps up and does something so out of the ordinary that it leaves you speechless. I saw an article about people who took courtesy to a whole new level. One person put a bunch of change in an envelope and taped it to a vending machine with a note: 'Get whatever you want on me!' Another person noticed some litter in a parking lot and walked around, picked it up and disposed of it. I could list story after story, but courtesy is one of the best gifts we can give to others. It may not be much in our mind, but to someone else it can be everything.

One last story on this subject—I want to share what happened after my wife and I had our first baby. The weather was getting nice and my wife started to take our daughter for a walk in the stroller around the pond by our home. Next to the pond there is some major construction going on and you can hear hammering, pounding, drilling and trucks working over there all day long. It can get quite loud. The path around the pond goes right by this construction area, however, the construction crew noticed my wife walking by with a baby and everyone stopped working, shut down the machines and didn't make any noise or start back up again until she had passed. Wow, that was cool! We never expected them to halt production for a few minutes so as not to upset a baby. That is just awesome! That is the gift of courtesy! It is a surprise, unexpected and means everything.

The Gift of Recharge

What drains our attitude of energy the most? Stress! Stress is caused by a number of things, changes at work, relationship issues, kids, moving, bills, money, annoying co-worker who likes to eat garlic for breakfast, family ... and the list can go on and on. Research shows that a little stress is good for you, but too much built up over time will eventually hurt you.

I am sitting at the airport as I write this and just looked up to see some guy is frantically scrambling to find a plug to charge in his cell phone. If you think about it, the phone that he is holding (or that you have) represents years of technological advancement. Millions – if not billions – of dollars were spent to develop the technology. However, if the cell phone doesn't have that little positive charge, it doesn't matter how much the technology cost, the phone will not do what it was designed to do. It's no good. The same is true for us. I've said it before; our attitude is much like a battery that needs to be recharged from time to time. The number one human attitude battery drainer is stress. When the stress builds up over time, it can lead to sickness and fatigue. Sometimes too much stress can lead to mental instability and poor decision making. Recharging your attitude is a maintenance process that leads to better emotional management.

If you are trying to give your best and are running on empty, your results will be less than average. Would you try running a marathon the day after a marathon? No way! If you did, you would not perform at your best. You need time to recharge. That is why I am always confused when organizations who want to turn a greater profit and boost productivity and performance don't take the time needed to do a little attitude maintenance. The biggest disservice to any bottom line, shareholders and maintaining a competitive edge is when the recharge process is overlooked or viewed with a very low appraisal. For years, there was a healthcare group that would hire me every year to speak to their employees and the reviews were always outstanding. Employees loved it and looked forward to it. Then the organization did some restructuring and leadership changed hands. The new person running the show was actually quoted as saying, "We are not wasting any more time on this attitude crap! People are lucky to have jobs in these times and if they don't want to work hard then they can leave."

Isn't that sad? Let me ask you, would you like to work for someone like that? Would you like to live with someone like that? This woman had a very low appraisal of attitude and soon it would get into the blood line of the company. As a result, there were more increased sick days from employees, more stress, higher turnover rate and a decline in customer service experiences.

When companies hire me to speak at their events or all-employee meetings, the purpose in mind is to recharge everyone's attitude batteries. You can't have high expectations or impose them upon others if there is no system in place to refuel energy, passion, purpose and enthusiasm. If your expectation is greatness, then you have got to do the simple things that make greatness possible.

When you value positive people engaged in positive action, you have to make the recharge process a significant priority. Whether your purpose is five days of intense training to discuss new changes to the company, talking shop, running numbers, training on new products, going over updated regulations, or planning for the future, there has to be a moment to fuel the attitude that drives people to make great things happen. An empty, stressed and fatigued attitude cannot win a worthwhile race. As a result, potential is never reached as far as it could be. So, the big question is how can you recharge your attitude batteries?

Recharging your attitude can be simple, fun and highly rewarding. It is more effective than pounding caffeine drinks all day. Don't get me wrong, I love my coffee, but recharging our attitude is what puts authentic and substantial fuel into your mental factory and we need that fuel to operate at our best. I will go into my 10 point attitude recharge plan in more depth in a later chapter. But for now, let me highlight a few simple and easy ways that work to recharge our attitude batteries.

Here are the most simple and relatively quick ideas to recharge your attitude batteries:

1. Go for a walk.
2. Take a 15 minute break to clear your mind, stretch, take a few deep breaths.
3. Read positive quotes.
4. Plan for more sleep at night or take a 20 minute nap. Did you know that Thomas Edison had a cot in his office and, when he felt like he needed a mental recharge, he would stop working and

take a short nap?

5. Get away. Plan a time to get away for a weekend or a few days and decompress by doing something fun for yourself.

6. Lighten up. Choosing to have a sense of humor is my favorite way to recharge and release stress.

I will highlight additional ways to enhance your attitude maintenance in a moment, but want to encourage you to get a note card and, on the front side, write at the top:

My Quick Recharges
1.
2.
3.
4.
5.

Then list 1 to 5 ways you can recharge your attitude within between 5 minutes and 30 minutes. The reason I suggest this is, when we get overly stressed, our mind isn't thinking at its best. The note card is a simple reminder of what works for you to get your attitude back on track. One person emailed me on Facebook and said, "I just got off the phone with a customer that screamed and chewed me out. It has really put a damper on my day. I feel like they just took every last fiber of my energy and positive attitude. What do you suggest to get my attitude back on track?"

I suggest the preplan recharge, which is identifying what works best for you. I can make suggestions, but you have to do what suits you best. The key is to ensure you are choosing healthy options to recharge your attitude. You don't want to put "Go eat a greasy football sized burrito and pound it with seven margaritas." While that may sound like fun to some, it's not the best way to maintain your mental stamina and strength. Think more simply, because the simple things are what do the best job.

Here is what I have on my note card:

1. Go to the coffee shop and chill.

2. Take the dogs for a 30 minute walk.

3. Watch a funny movie.

4. Talk with my wife

5. Take a 20 minute nap.

6. Prank phone call my brothers.

That last one was a bonus one, but I do get a good laugh and kick out of calling them and messing with them a little.

On the other side of the note card, write this down at the top:

MY BIG RECHARGE:

" _____ "

This is something that maybe you will do once a year. It is your time to do what you want and recharge your way. It could be a vacation to a beach, visit relatives, take a cruise… it's whatever you want. If you have the budget and can plan for it, do it.

I like to visit my parents who live on a lake to

spend time fishing and sleeping. That is literally all I do, fish and sleep. I take so many naps that people have to nudge me to see if I am still alive. But this is what recharges me. I forget about work and let the stress go, so when I go home I am recharged to give my best to my family, myself, my work and my customers.

One affordable workplace idea is to get a video of your favorite speaker and play it at a meeting. I prefer one that can mix humor and quality content.

A few years ago, I won some pretty cool awards for The Most Outstanding Motivational Video. I am proud of that because I wanted to make something that actually held people's attention, so making them was going against the current of everything out there. But, it worked. And the reason why I was able to make a great tool that people can use to recharge in the workplace is because I know what it is like to sit through meetings when you are sitting there physically, but sitting somewhere else on a beach drinking a cool beverage mentally. Do you know what

I mean? Yeah you do! I have Attention Deficit Disorder and so my mind will drift to whatever is the most captivating in the moment. I remember sitting in meetings to discuss plans about future meetings or debrief about past meetings. Talk about torture... Or how about that one guy who calls a meeting just so he can talk, talk, talk and hear his own voice? Yeah—you know that guy! I used to dread meetings so much that I actually tried to get a note from the doctor to say I had bladder problems and would not be able to sit through a lot of meetings. I was unsuccessful in obtaining that note, but I would bring in a big gulp from 7-11, which is like a gallon of soda, put it in front of me and drink it all during the meeting. When I felt it was time to go, I would smile, start to get up and when everyone looked to see where I was going, I would just shake the bathtub size cup as a visual reason for my exiting the meeting. Everyone just smiled and nodded in agreement. It was my perfect out, until others started catching on and doing the same. *Grrrr!*

I think what ties up a meeting really well or kicks it off is something uplifting and inspirational. Even if it is a budget meeting, end it or start it with something uplifting. Most people I know need something uplifting after budget meetings. This is the most wallet friendly idea to recharge people in the workplace. But, it not only recharges you in the workplace, it expands into your personal life as well. I have a few videos I like to watch at my desk that have me bursting with laughter and that recharge my attitude. Now, I am not suggesting you sit at your desk and watch funny videos. I own the company, so I get that privilege, but I only do it for a few minutes to recharge my attitude. I am not sitting there for hours posting funny cat videos on Facebook. I have the intent to watch a video clip or two and, after I watch them, I feel great! One of my favorite comedians and someone who I am often compared to is Brian Regan. I personally think we both have our own uniqueness, but, as a special recharge gift, I took my friends, family and staff to see Brian at Zanies Comedy Club, and to surprise them all, I took them backstage to meet Brian. They loved it and it was a total recharge for them, but I notice when they watch his stuff they get that perk and positive step in their attitude.

So, how valuable is an attitude recharge? You may be able to relate to this woman I encountered while shopping. I had an interesting experience a few months ago, it was great feedback as to how much people need an attitude recharge. I was waiting in line at the Meijer's pharmacy and out of the corner of my eye noticed some woman staring at me. I didn't make eye contact, but I did that face brush with my hand to make sure there was nothing on my face or hanging from my nose. I just played on my phone while I was waiting and, out of the corner of my eye, I could see her stepping towards me to get my attention. She tapped me on the arm with a smile, "I know who you are." My eyes perked up as my eyebrows rose a little in curiosity.

"You do … do you?"

"My work showed one of your videos at a

meeting. You fell off an airplane and you had your underwear taped to your luggage. Is that you?"

With everyone in the pharmacy area now looking directly at me, I smiled, "Ummm… Yep that would be me."

"Our department played one of your videos at a meeting and I was, like, you look so familiar. I didn't mean to bother you, but I wanted to tell you that we enjoyed watching your videos."

"Thank you, it is no bother. How did you guys hear about me?"

"One of my co-workers saw you speak at a conference a few years ago and she brought your videos to work. I don't think I have ever seen everyone laugh like that before. That doesn't happen often. One guy laughed so hard he spilled his coffee everywhere and just about fell out of his chair. We needed that. We have been going through a lot of changes, growth, and it is incredibly stressful. I have a supervisor who makes everyone's life very difficult and there are times I have gotten physically sick because of it. But sometimes we just need a little something positive to help us out."

If you want to boost personal and professional enthusiasm and energy, start by recharging your attitude and the attitudes around you. Don't force it on people because they may not be used to it, but make the effort to incorporate the gift of recharge into your culture so people begin to accept and appreciate it more. Who knew that little mental break would put so much fuel and energy into our greatest asset—our attitude!

The Gift of Recognition

Recognition makes people feel like rock stars. Everyone wants to know that who they are and what they do matters. One of the most empowering ways to put a positive spark in someone's attitude is to give them the gift of attitude by acknowledging them. People are so hungry for the sound of recognition and praise that they will climb buildings to fill the need. I recall reading an article about some guy who was arrested for climbing city buildings. They called him The Human Spider-man. People would cheer him on while he climbed and, when interviewed as to what his motivation was for doing something so crazy, his response was "I just wanted to hear the cheers."

Recognition gives people a sense of purpose in that what they are doing truly matters. Recognition is simply acknowledging the value of others and the things they do. People want to know that progress is happening because of them. They want to feel involved and a part of something worthwhile. Years ago, as I was doing a sound check for a speaking engagement, there was a young man named Curtis there who had volunteered to help me set up. We worked together for about an hour. When we were done, I told him, "Curtis, you keep doing what you do. You are a rock star! Thank you so much for your time and effort in helping me get all set up today."

He looked away to hide the tears that were building up and I inquired, "Hey… You okay, man? Do I smell bad or something?"

"Yes, I am okay. But you are the first person ever to thank and compliment me on my work around here.

That just means so much to me."

Another time, when I got home from a long trip, I made my way into the kitchen to grab a light snack and sit down to decompress a little. It was close to 1am and I was trying to be quiet so the dogs wouldn't bark and wake up everyone in the house and neighborhood. When I opened up our pantry I was in shock. My first thought was, "Oh boy, I am so tired, I think I am in someone else's house!!"

The pantry didn't look familiar at all. I stepped back and looked around to make sure I was in the right house because you never know. Crazier things have happened to me. Yep, it was the right house, but what had happened to the pantry? It looked like it had been overhauled. Someone had made it look nice. Before, you didn't know what was in there and some things possibly dated back to when Abraham Lincoln was elected President. At times, my wife and I get busy and so things accumulate and a house pantry can take on a life of its own. I stopped going in there out of fear that something might jump out and get me. But this particular night, I wanted to see if we had some crackers and, when I opened it up, it looked like the pantry fairy came and gave us the gift of a clean pantry and fresh, edible food.

I didn't ask my wife to clean the pantry, because why should it be any more her job than mine? We have stuff going on and it wasn't the highest thing to do on our priority list. I just kind of figured that, at some point, the pantry would get so bad that we would just move or invite people over for a pantry cleaning party. That way we could share the fun.

She had spent hours cleaning it and it looked amazing. If I could show you a before and after picture here, your mouth would drop. I am serious, it was incredible work. After I showed up, cleaned up and started to crawl into bed, I realized I was in the wrong house when I there were other people in my bed! *Just kidding. Gotcha. Just making sure you are still with me.* My wife and I did that quiet whispering chit chat you do in the dark, "How was your event, honey?"

"It was good. Glad to be home."

And then I quietly said, "Babe, the pantry looks amazing. You did such a great job. Thank you for doing that."

She perked up, leaned over, smiled big. "You noticed?!! That means so much."

"YES, I noticed. That was amazing of you to take the time to do that. For real. Thank you."

I am sure it wasn't fun for her to spend all that time cleaning the pantry when she had so many other things going on, but when I recognized her for doing it, it made it all worth it. She didn't care about how long it took, or having to haul heavy trash bags to the garage, but what made it 100% worth it to her was that little recognition.

Recognition in a relationship is so vital to the growth of that relationship. It is a form of love that deepens the quality and connection of that relationship. My wife cheers and throws a party for me whenever I change out a roll of toilet paper and put on a new roll. It doesn't seem like a big deal to me, but apparently it is to her. There are other things I do around our house that I just figure need to get done, so I do them. And my wife will write me a little note of thanks and share with me reasons why she loves me. Her recognition makes me feel special and that is what recognition is all about. It is a gift.

Recognition works with others when you are out and about running errands. The other day, someone held a door open for me. I praised this person by saying, "Thank you, I love when people are so nice as to hold the door for others." He smiled and accepted the praise. But guess what he will do and be happy to do again? Hold the door for someone else. Why? Because of the praise and recognition.

Extraordinary Leadership Makes Recognition Priority #1

I was checking in at the American Airlines desk in Indianapolis, and everyone seemed happy and chipper behind the counter. That is, until I overheard one of the employees telling another, "Nate is working this shift with us today." After she said that, it was like you could see life draining out of everyone. Smiles faded, and I think I even saw someone begin to slouch. I thought to myself, "Who is this Nate that nobody is happy to work with?"

The woman continued to vent, "All he ever does is look over our shoulder and correct us on stuff all day long."

Based on the information I was hearing, I might categorize Nate as a classic micro-manager. He doesn't trust others do their job, so exerts extra energy on his part to overlook and correct everyone's efforts. It is uncomfortable for Nate to let people do what they were hired to do, so he is always observing what isn't done right.

I am assuming that that Nate wasn't the most respected person by his peers and I only suggest that based on the verbal bashing he was receiving from them. I could hear it. They were not holding back anything. I am a customer listing to this and thinking, *I sure would not want to work with Nate or for Nate*.

The remedy for Nate's insecurities or shortcomings as leader involves some simple modifications. However, nobody can choose to do that but Nate. That is Nate's job as it is our job in our own situations. It's clear that Nate has a seat at the leadership table, but if he wants to stay, he has to make some upgrades to his current leadership style.

Leaders should always be trying to improve and open to feedback that will help them improve. The 'My way or the highway' leadership style just won't work to achieve long term success.

My bet is that Nate was not the best at recognition. He may have some great strengths that we – the customers – didn't hear his peers mention as they were verbally bashing him behind his back. Maybe Nate never got recognized himself and wasn't exactly familiar with how it works. Maybe he just didn't make recognition a priority because it wasn't in his job description to do so. Leaders who choose to recognize others for their efforts, attitudes and progress do so not because they have to or it's required, but because they understand that, when people feel valued and important, they are more positively engaged in the workplace.

It may not happen overnight, but if you start small and build your recognition sense, you will begin to see what a difference it makes. My advice: Don't copy Nate's leadership style. Rather, make it a part of your leadership process to start looking for the good in others, and reinforce positive behavior with authentic praise and recognition.

A little praise and recognition can go a long way. Be on the lookout for things your kids are doing well at and point it out to them. Do the same for your significant other. Recognize the lady at the coffee shop, "Thank you for always having such a super smile when I come in to start my day."

Recognize and praise your co-workers, "Frank, thanks for not eating garlic anymore, the office seems to smell so much better."

It can be anything. If you make people feel special and acknowledge their best efforts and communicate that, because of them, progress is the result, you will master the gift of recognition. Remember, everyone hungers for it. If you make it a priority to recognize and praise someone for something, you will begin to start looking more and more for what is right in others and circumstances versus what is wrong and not working. That is what attitude is all about.

The Gift of
Encouragement

Our late president, Richard M. Nixon, after leaving the White House to resign from the highest office in the land, was so discouraged and depressed that he was actually admitted to a hospital. Filled with despair, he told his wife while in the hospital: "Patricia, I am so depressed, I wish God would let me die."

At that very moment, a nurse entered the room with a cheery smile and said, "Mr. President, have you looked out the window today?"

He was so filled with sadness that he had let his family, his country and himself down that he intentionally kept the curtains closed—refusing to allow any sunlight in. She said, "We really need to let some light in here, so that may cheer you up."

She went to the window, opened the curtains, and at that very moment a plane flew across the sky with an advertising banner behind it (similar to what you would see at the ocean in the summer). The sign simply said:

"Mr. President, God loves you and we do too."

Tears began streaming down the former Commander in Chief's cheeks. He said, "How long has that plane been flying today?"

The nurse said, "Matter of fact, it has been flying back and forth all day." The woman who rented the plane told the pilot to keep flying back and forth in front of the hospital until he noticed the curtains in his room open. In case you are wondering who paid for the banner? It was Ruth Bell Graham (Dr. Billy's Graham's wife).

Something awesome happens when we get connected to a little encouragement. It makes us feel better about life and ourselves. Encouragement really feeds us strength to stop thinking down and start thinking up. We gain confidence so that we can tackle the biggest giants in our life. Encouragement comes in different forms at different times.

Encouragement feeds our attitude with renewed inspiration and energy. It opens our minds to find solutions where we thought there were none. Sometimes, people need just a little dose of encouragement to keep moving forward.

In high school, basketball was my life. My parents had to buy three basketball backboards and rims because we played so much we just wore them out. In the summer, it didn't matter how hot and humid it was, me, my brothers and the neighbors would just keep playing basketball all day. Dad would get upset with us because we kept running in and out of the house, slamming doors so we could get a drink of water. Finally, they got us water coolers and that cut back on the running in and out of the house, unless we had to use the rest room. In the summer months, we weren't allowed to sit inside and play video games or watch TV. It was a rule that we had to be doing something and basketball was our choice of activity.

As my love for the game grew, I had the good fortune to attend several basketball camps and improve my skills. I would play pick-up games wherever I could find one going on. Sometimes when my brothers and friends would get tired of playing the game, I would challenge them, "If you can beat me at one on one, I will give you $5." I never lost. Not because I was the greatest player in the world, but mostly because I didn't have $5 to give away. Any money I did get, I would buy basketball magazines, cut out the pictures of great players and post them all over my bedroom walls. I did that because it inspired me to keep working hard so that, one day, I could play ball at the same level as them.

My passion for the game did have a few drawbacks, a major one being the smell after practice. At one point, my brother walked in my room and said, "Hey man, your room smells like a nasty basketball shoe or like some fish died in here." I got home from basketball practice one night and was so tired that I didn't even shower. I didn't even get out of my practice clothes that were quite ripe with an odor that wasn't pleasant for any human. I was so tired I fell on my bed and literally passed out. I woke up the next day, saw that I was still in my stinky clothes and thought, "Oh man, I am going to have to burn or bury the blankets on my bed to get this gross and nasty smell out of here."

Going into my senior year in high school, I had such incredible ambition and expectation for a basketball scholarship. Since the scores on my ACT college prep test were below my shoe size, I knew I wouldn't be getting any academic scholarships to Yale or Brown anytime soon. History was my favorite class and subject and there wasn't much about history on these tests.

I was invited to play a private game of basketball with some college and pro players at Northern Iowa University in the Dome and a few college coaches were there to observe. I was so excited to be there and I held my own. I hustled. I passed the ball. I rebounded. I was on my game, and then I was about to do something for the highlight reel. I got a steal and began a fast break to the basket. Nobody was around me, so I jumped and for a moment I kind of felt like Peter Pan. It was my best leap ever. I slammed the ball through the hoop with authority. The backboard made some old man noises, but it was a thunderous slam dunk.

My only challenge was, I knew how to jump really well, but hadn't quite perfected my landing. I would jump as high as I could go and sometimes just land flat on my back or face because of how I landed. I figured in time I would master my balance and get some landing gear that worked for me. But, this time my landing was not good. I hurt my knee and bad. I would rather not to explain the details of the injury because, even though it is over 25 years since that happened, it still gives me the willies to think about. That is why I hate when I watch sports on TV and if someone gets hurt they keep replaying it over and over. That drives me nuts. This time, as I lay flat on my back looking up at the basketball rim, I knew something was not right. I couldn't walk. My knee was not bending right. They had to help me off the court and the player I once was would never be again. The injury wasn't a career ending injury, but it did a little more than hurt my physical body, it hurt my attitude, hopes, dreams and ambitions.

My parents took me to a few doctors and one wanted to operate, but I wasn't ready for that kind of procedure and wanted to see if I had any other options. One doctor suggested some aggressive physical therapy. So we opted for the physical therapy, but the only hiccup was I would have to wear a special knee brace. It was expensive and would be designed specifically for my knee. They had to do a mold of my entire leg in order to construct the brace. When I went to try on the brace for the first time, it was nearly the size of my whole leg. It felt weird and uncomfortable. What I thought would help me started to become a mental doubt. The brace limited my mobility and speed, but it kept my knee stable enough so no further damage would happen.

As hard as I tried to stay positive, it wasn't easy. I worked as hard as I could to be the same player I was before the injury, but I couldn't make it happen. My performance on the basketball court was less than spectacular. I could no longer jump as high. College coaches stopped calling my house to recruit me. It was like everything was going south and drying up overnight.

I found myself feeling more and more depressed. It was still my senior year, early part of the season, and I thought about quitting. I got benched twice already and my playing time was being reduced. It felt humiliating and I knew that I should be a good teammate, but it was hard to do that when I knew my dream was draining like water in a sink.

It was about the 6th game into the season—Friday night game night. I used to live for those nights. I would be so excited and our entire house just lived for these games. My parents would let me take the second car we had and drive to the school early so I could warm up and get ready. I had taken a short nap before I had to go and when I woke up, I put my face into my pillow and started to cry and let out the pain that was weighing me down. I didn't want anyone to come into my room and see me blubbering into a pillow, so I tried crying as quietly as I could.

I got off the bed, looked in the mirror and my eyes were red. I was trying to think of excuses to explain why. "I was cutting up onions in my room."

I sat at the bottom of the bed and began to feel even worse because my mom and dad used money they didn't have to send me to camps, pay for physical therapy and get me the knee brace. They didn't say anything about it, but I could just feel that they felt a little broken by all this because they shared my ambitions as well.

I stood up off the bed and started to get dressed, but I noticed there was an envelope on one of my pillows. I almost didn't see it, but it was a card from my mom. I opened it and read some of the most beautiful words of encouragement that I have ever known in this life. The card closed with these words, "Samuel, we love you and we believe in you. Now is the time for you to believe in yourself."

I got goose bumps as I read those words filled with such life. At that moment, I took a deep breath and it was all the encouragement I needed to flush out my toxic thinking and pull me out of a pity party. I got dressed and made my way to the school to get ready for the game. The gym was packed, the band was playing and it was loud. For the first time in my varsity career my coach did not start me. It was humbling, but something in me was different. The game started and, in a matter of three minutes, our team was down by nearly 12 points and looking awful. My coach looked frustrated and kept looking down the bench at me and I just looked back at him lifting my eyebrows as a signal, *Put me in!*

He looked down at me again and said, "Well?!

Are you ready to do something?!"

I said, "Yes, sir!"

"WELL THEN...GET IN THERE, SAMMM!"

I checked into the game at the next break and I am not saying this to boast or exaggerate (maybe a little), but I did something I had never done in the game of basketball before – I dominated! I was no longer the player I used to be, but I was the best player I could become. I adapted to the unexpected change in my life and learned ways to play the game smarter. I didn't try to win every game by myself or focus only on my stats and how many points I scored. I worked with my team and they worked with me. It was a unified effort and we encouraged each other to keep going in the good and rough times. When one man wasn't playing his best, we would lift him up. We functioned as one and I learned apart of the game that I hadn't known before.

At the end of the season, I had the privilege and honor of being named to the All Conference Team. I was the number one rebounder and ended up getting a full ride basketball scholarship. While, college ball proved to be fun and challenging, new injuries continued to mount until it become quite evident that it was time to hang up the smelly basketball shoes for good. I was at peace in doing so. I had a great moment in time and have no regrets, but only lessons. I had had an experience that I will never forget. But, the most monumental part of that journey which sticks with me the most is the encouragement I received that gave me new hope, filled me with a rekindled enthusiasm and fueled my strength to fight back and achieve my goals.

Everyone needs a little encouragement from time to time. It doesn't mean we are weak. It means we need some fuel to keep going, get better and reach our best. Some days, I could use a lot of it! One time, when I was really in the dumps mentally, I thought about going to the Hallmark store and reading every "pick me up" card to see if the words in the cards would actually pick up my droopy attitude. Oddly enough, I just ate some peanut butter and life was all better again.

You see, encouragement can be a few simple words shared from the heart, an extended hand to help someone out or a small act of kindness that communicates the most uplifting and empowering message anyone and everyone desires to hear, and that is... *"Everything will be okay."*

Sam Glenn

The Gift of

Negativity

I say this with the utmost level of enthusiasm— let's talk about negative stuff! Is there any real gift or good that can come from negativity? Since I used to be a very negative person, I happen to have some credible firsthand experience on this subject. Negativity is like a disgruntled employee who doesn't care, makes circumstances worse and ends up costing the company a fortune. When you observe negativity or drama, it becomes a teachable example of what not to do and what doesn't work. We can learn from that and apply the lessons.

The consequence of negativity in life and the workplace is you lose customers, you reduce your chances for new opportunities like promotions and bonuses, you treat others poorly and you engage in unhealthy habits. And finally, the biggest consequence of a negative attitude is that it's just ugly. And that isn't my opinion, but rather a fact.

An ugly attitude does not have your best interests at hand. It doesn't work for you. Have you ever seen an adult throw a temper tantrum fueled with drama and thought, *How is that going to help them or make their situation better?* It won't. The wrong attitude just doesn't work to make happen what you want to happen. I know, I have tried and tried and tried.

A few years ago, I was on a conference call with a company that was inquiring about having me speak at their annual conference. They had five different people from their company on the call. I am not a big fan of conference calls. I think they take up unnecessary time, create confusion and really distort quality communication. I was leaning forward at my desk trying to hear everyone talk over each other and it literally felt like I was working at a McDonald's drive through and a van of crazy teenagers pulled up and were shouting over each other what they wanted. I spent over an hour listening to them while I played with Play-doh on my desk. If you have ADD (Attention Deficit Disorder) like me, a meeting like this can be a little bit torturous. I had to work hard to stay focused and figure out who was saying what and answer questions being thrown at me from every direction. When they started asking me questions, I felt like a grilled cheese sandwich. They were grilling me on everything.

One lady sternly asked, "Mr. Glenn, this is Paula. Sorry for the background noise, but my question to you is do you just tell people to think and be positive and everything will be good? Because our company is more than just about being positive."

Now, in situations like this, I would actually talk the group out of booking me and suggest some other speaker that would be a better fit. I did this once and one lady said to me, "You are the first speaker I have ever talked to that wasn't trying to be all things and suggested other speakers instead of yourself"

Well, it's true. If I don't feel like I am a good fit, or that it is win/win situation, then I will pass on the business. I love new business, but I like the right business. I don't like putting myself in a situation that no matter how hard I work there is no realistic way I will meet their expectation – which might also be multiple expectations based on the situation I am sharing right now. It doesn't matter how much they pay, it just isn't worth the time and stress, so I will pass on the speaking opportunity. The woman was correct when she said that a lot of speakers will try to be all things to all clients because they want the business. Most will, but the good ones won't. I believe there is room to adapt and develop to make your stuff work for a client, but I absolutely refuse to be and do someone that I am not. That would be unfair to everyone. My priority is to give my best at all times, but if I am put in a situation that could potentially dilute my best, I will pass. My goal is to shine, not be dulled.

So in this particular case, I suggested it might be good to wait until they saw me at a conference or heard more about my work in the media. Most of my work is word of mount anyway, so the reason I make this suggestion to some groups is so they can see me in action, the response of the audience and how happy I made my client. This avenue will give them concrete confidence in booking me. The funny part was that the reason they were contacting me was that someone did see me at a conference and highly recommended me for their event. Despite my best efforts to get them excited about another speaker or waiting until they learn more about me down the road - they were insistent that they definitely wanted me. They wanted something customized to their audience, and later I learned the reason they were so intense on interviewing me is they had a few poor experiences with speakers in the past and wanted to ensure they would not repeat that mistake

As I was talking about the purpose of my attitude speeches, I got the vibe they were not grasping the true value of it. The one lady cut me off mid-sentence, "Mr. Glenn, we know you speak on attitude, but we are not looking for a Rah Rah pep talk. We are looking for substance and content. What value or effect will your message have on our people and organization?"

So I began to explain to the five people on the conference call that my message sounds a lot more lightweight than it really is. In fact, the other day I read an article about another professional speaker making fun of speakers who talk about attitude. Maybe it was to build his stuff up, but in any case I just laugh and shake my head when I read junk like that. When you have to put others down in an attempt to make your stuff shine, it shows a lack of class.

My philosophy is that it all starts with attitude. The success and culture of an organization is driven and determined by attitude. The growth, leadership and future of an organization depend on attitude.

Attitude is what drives innovation, possibilities and new ideas. Attitude is our emotional management center that determines how we handle stress, pressure and respond to change. Our attitude influences our level of effort and the choices we make. So, I think it would be fair to say attitude is kind of a big deal.

The conference call was a little overwhelming and I wanted to assist them to understand what I do better and the real depth of my materials, so I decided to share with everyone on the call an epic story that featured a confrontational adventure between me and a store manager. I wanted to highlight the costs and consequences of negative attitudes in the workplace and this story was an excellent illustration of that. There is a bigger picture when it comes to this attitude stuff. However, it's unfortunate how expensive the costs can add up to be when any size organization doesn't make attitude a top priority. The following story is about how we can learn and gain something positive from something negative. After I shared this story, the group hired me. They connected to the bigger picture of what I was trying to get them to see. And, I would add, they turned out to be a fantastic organization to work with, great people and they continue to have me back to speak, without as much grilling.

Everyone,
Meet Manager Mike

I had a cash budget of $500 and wanted to get a second TV for the house. My wife and I discussed it and were set on only spending $500. It was my job to make it happen, so I decided to go to a store that is known for their competitive prices. I felt like I might get the best deal there so that is where I went. When I got to the electronics section and saw all the different kinds of televisions on display, I drew a blank. I was dumbfounded. I didn't know the first thing about TVs. There were so many options, sizes, HD, 3D, plasma…

The sales associate, who appeared to still be in high school, was actually very helpful and gave me some suggestions. That is when my eye spotted the good deal—an open box sale. An open box is perhaps a returned item, discontinued or the last one in stock. The open box item was marked down a few hundred dollars, so it was a good deal. However, the price on this particular open box television was about $50 above my budget. Now, I grew up knowing that it never hurts to ask for a better price. So I asked the sales associate if they could discount a little more to help me meet my budget. She informed that she could not make that decision and would call her manager to see if he could come and approve the additional discount.

She paged her manager and 15 minutes went by. I cracked a joke, "Is he on his lunch break?"

She said she would try paging him again. Another 10 minutes went by before a very stern individual came around the corner of the aisle. If we slowed down the picture and captioned his walk towards me, he looked like I interrupted his favorite television show and was not happy. He had no smile on his face. He didn't make eye contact. He seemed annoyed and the first words out of his mouth to the customer holding $500 cash were, "What seems to be the problem?"

The younger sales associate spoke up, "There is no problem. This gentleman would like to buy a TV today and only has a budget of $500. He would like this open box TV, but was wondering if you could work with his budget and discount it a bit more?"

A whole two seconds went by for the store manager to think about the question before he responded, "Absolutely not. This item has already been marked down." And without saying another word, he began to walk away. I came for a TV and ended up in a real life drama. Since I was the customer holding the cash, I figured I was the main character in this story, but according to the store manager and how he treated me, I was simply an extra who wasn't even worthy of kindness.

But, you see, as a customer I don't tolerate that kind of behavior, nor should you. I didn't need to be treated with such a production of drama. Would you accept that? All he had to do was say "No". I would have accepted that. His display of negativity was about to become a gift. I am sharing that gift with you right now. He showed us what doesn't work. He showed us how to make his organization look bad. He showed us how to be a poor leader. He showed that he didn't care. He showed us how to lose customers. He gave us the gift of negativity.

Before he got more than 10 feet away, I pleasantly called out to him, "Excuse me, sir!"

He quickly turned and had a look that said if his eyes could shoot laser beams, this drama would be upgraded to a blockbuster, "Yes?!"

I inquired, "I was wondering what your name was?"

He pointed to his name tag, "My name is manager Mike!"

"Hi manager Mike, I am Sam Glenn, the

customer. I have to say the way you treated me just now wasn't a great experience. Instead of acknowledging my presence, you made me feel like a problem. I am a loyal customer and think you could have done a little better today in how you addressed this situation."

His look grew darker and his face turned red, not from being embarrassed by his attitude and actions, but because his inner rage was inching out. He stared me down in silence for what was a few awkward and long seconds. I wasn't about to say anything. It was his turn to talk. What do you have to say about being called out about your rude behavior?

"Sir, I am busy and don't have time for this."

"You mean time to treat a customer like they are the reason you are in business. I forgot, I thought I was the one holding the cash?"

"Sir, I am not going to get into this with you. If you want the open box television, it's the price listed. Otherwise, stop wasting my time."

He didn't get it. This epic showdown wasn't about

the price of the television. They had another TV that I was planning on getting if they didn't reduce the cost on the open box. This was about attitude. I didn't want to keep going back and forth with him, because he was not open to reason or understanding. He was stuck in his attitude and wasn't willing to budge. The sales associate, who was standing about a foot away from me, had this look of terror on her face like she could not believe someone was standing up to her store manager and his attitude. This would be a good lesson for her—what not to do.

So, I wrapped up our confrontational adventure with "Well, Manager Mike, this was very disappointing. I am disappointed in your performance today. If this was America's Got Talent, you would have gotten "Xs" from all the judges and booed off the stage."

He glared at me and tightened up his lips, shook his head and walked away. The young sales associate looked up and said, "I love that show!"

I smiled back, "I do too, but unfortunately, I won't

be watching it on a television from your store. You just don't treat customers the way he just treated me. Does he always act that way?"

She nodded up and down, "Yeah, he is in a bad mood every day. I am really sorry about that."

"Well remember this, when you treat customers like he treated me, you lose everything you really want."

So how do we extract something positive from this negative story? Let's do a little math and determine the total costs of the store manager's poor attitude.

a. Did manager Mike make his company look good?

b. Did manager Mike turn a potential customer into a loyal customer?

c. Did manager Mike make himself look good?

d. Did manager Mike make his company a profit?

e. Did manager Mike create an experience that would turn into a referral business—would I tell people to shop there?

f. Did Manager Mike not pay attention during

company paid training? (Hmmmm...)

What if we took the math another way, a way we all can relate to? Let's say one customer with $500 walks into Manager Mike's store every day for a year. We will call that customer Sam. Based on manager Mike's attitude, we can probably assume that the customer (Sam) will opt out of spending that $500 in his store. So if we take one $500 customer x 365 days = $182,500 a year in lost business.

How would you feel if you knew your company lost that much in a year all due to someone's attitude? But, let's take it another step further. This particular store where manager Mike works is a national retail chain with close to 6000 stores. What if one negative employee at each store location treated one customer with $500 to spend the same way manager Mike treated me for one day?

I will let you do the math: $500 customer x 11,000 stores x 1 day of the year = $5,500,000.

If you lost 5 million bucks, would you be a happy

camper? Would you invest a little extra time, effort and resources into fixing the problem?

Take a look at the math if one customer a day with just $50 to spend is treated poorly everyday for a year and takes that $50 to spend elsewhere.

1 Customer with $50 to spend x

365 days in a year = $18,250 x

1 negative employee per stoer   x

11, 000 stores =

Grand Total in Lost Business: $200,750,000

Anyone think revaluating things based on attitude is a good idea?

WOW! How insane is that number in lost revenue? Is it a realistic number? Well, that is conservatively calculating only 365 dissatisfied customers at one location a year and one negative employee doing a bad job. The customer has the right to fire an entire company based on their experiences. If you have people creating enough of the wrong ones, can you image how the number in lost revenue would increase? Are you beginning to see how having the wrong attitude can cost you everything you want? What is the consequence of having the wrong attitude? Just do the math. It is the one math problem that is the most overlooked in the boardroom or a share holders meeting. Think about it.

The big picture is we can learn from negativity. We can learn what doesn't work and that is the gift of negativity.

What would have worked better for manager Mike? I think the solution is quite simple. Here are 5 of my personal suggestions:

1. *Choose a better attitude.*

2. *Make eye contact and a smile.*

3. *Listen.*

4. *Try and understand the situation from the customer's perspective – put yourself in their shoes and ask yourself how you would want to be treated. Be a problem solver. You can either*

make something better or worse. A problem solver will demonstrate effort and a willingness to try and help. Tell the customer "Let me see what I can do." And even if you can't do anything, most will be pleased that you at least tried to do something on their behalf.

The gift of attitude given to customers is uncomplicated if you do a few little things really well. Eventually, those little things become your greatest strengths. Unfortunately, manager Mike made the choice to complicate something so simple and the consequence of his negativity that led to unnecessary drama became an expense to his organization and a liability to his leadership example. Take mental notes of what doesn't work and do not do it.

Sam Glenn

The Gift of
Moving Forward

Sometimes things happen that bring a halt to everything. It's called unexpected change. Change is uncomfortable; it is inconvenient and takes time to adapt to. I heard a saying that change is inevitable, but growth is optional. I love reading stories about people who faced the odds with courage and came out ahead. They found a way to keep moving forward when everything thrown at them became a roadblock or set back. Instead of giving up, throwing in the towel, they get that 'keep moving forward' attitude and as a result they start to see renewed possibilities

121

for their life and circumstances. I particularly love the story of a woman who ran a successful hair salon.

One day, a national chain built a salon just across the street. She could have complained, "What if they put me out of business? What will I do?" However, she decided to keep the right attitude. When the salon across the street opened, they had a big sign in the window that said, 'Special—$5 Haircuts!' The woman responded with the right attitude—and it brought her more business. She put a sign in her window that said, 'We fix $5 haircuts!'

I recall a time before my speaking career took off when I wasn't sure if anyone would ever call to have me speak. It had been a whole year of putting the word out there and nobody was calling. My 'keep moving forward' tank was starting to run on empty. I could hear the sounds of doubt and fear knocking at the door. I was just about out of money and still nobody was calling. I put everything on the line to make my dream – of becoming an author and a nationally recognized speaker on the subject of attitude – a reality. I would pace in front of the answering machine, checking it up to 10 times an hour to see if anyone had called. I must have heard over 100 times a day, "You have no new voicemails."

I began to question myself, *What am I doing wrong? Maybe I am not good enough. How am I going to make it if I fail? All I need is a chance.*

I was on the edge of giving up. I didn't have any more strength to keep moving forward. One night, I noticed a present on the kitchen table with my name on it. It was from a friend who believed in me and knew I needed some 'keep moving forward' fuel. The gift was a book by Dr. Robert Schuller, ***Tough Times Don't Last, But Tough People Do***. It was autographed as well. I flipped through the pages and wedged between several pages was $300 cash. I was floored by such a generous gift and it wasn't so much the money or the book that inspired me, it was the message of the gift. My friend's confidence in who I was and what I was doing inspired me to keep moving forward. It gave me hope to hold on and not to give up. I was on the edge of giving up so many times. Now, no matter what type of group I speak for, I know it would not have happened or become real had I stopped moving forward. But I couldn't have done it alone. When I was weak and out of ideas, the encouragement from loved ones inspired me to keep moving forward—to keep pressing on. Too often there is a fight that is going on inside us. A part of us wants to throw in the towel and quit and the other part is saying with every last fiber, *Just a little further*.

Life is always going to throw us curve balls and change ups that throw everything off course. It is in those moments we can start to fill up with doubts, but those are the times we have to find the fire to fuel the fire to keep moving forward. We can learn from the stories of those in history who faced outstanding challenges, but somehow and someway they found a way. The underlying factor was they kept moving forward. Let those lessons be fuel to inspire you to keep moving forward as well.

The Gift of
Integrity

Have you ever been burned by someone due to their lack of truthfulness? I am going to assume yes. It hurts and weakens the bridge of trust. It ends relationships. It crushes credibility in an instant. Integrity is about communicating through your actions and attitude in such a way that people trust you. Maybe you are like me and at times have said out loud, "Who can you trust these days?" When people break the bond of honesty, it shifts your thinking to *who can I trust?* A little truthfulness goes a long way.

We had just moved to a new state and were basically starting over from scratch. One of my priorities was to get established and set up with a new accountant. That was my job. I did some Google searching, made calls, sent emails and interviewed a few to see who would be a good fit for my company. After some careful consideration, I was able to narrow it down to someone I thought would have my business and family's best interests at heart. I didn't just want bookkeeping services, but someone who would work well with our goals for the future. My initial conversation with the accountant I picked had me feeling secure that I had made a good choice. However, the thing about integrity is that it entails much more than our words. Our integrity also reveals its true nature in our actions, choices and behaviors. Some people try to bend the bar of integrity to justify certain actions, and integrity doesn't work that way. When you do what is right, communicate truthfully and do what you say you will do when you say you will—that is what integrity is in motion.

I thought, as a friendly gesture, I would stop into my new accountant's office for a quick visit to introduce my wife and new baby girl. I wanted them to know who my family was and how important they are to me. Plus, I wanted to get my wife's official nod that I had picked someone who would work with what we needed. So, I called them up to find a good time to pop in when it wasn't too busy for them, so they could meet my family. The visit would be only for a few minutes. They expressed excitement for us to stop in and so the family got into the car and made the five minute ride to their office.

Now, before I continue with our family visit to the new accountant's office, I should give you a little history about me and office visits. When I was growing up, my mom would do something that made you think you died and went to heaven first class. My brothers and I would be upstairs playing with our favorite toy – LEGO! – and as we would be building Lego creations from our imagination, we would hear pans being pulled out in the kitchen. "MOM IS BAKING COOKIES!!!"

Have you ever seen dogs go insane when the doorbell rings or someone is knocking at the door? That describes me and my brothers rushing down the stairs, pushing each other over and fighting to get to the kitchen to see if we could help Mom bake. The reason we liked to help bake is that, as helpers, we got to try everything and eat a bunch of samples or cookies if Mom didn't like how they turned out. I didn't care how they turned out, it was a cookie and my stomach doesn't know the difference. It loves cookies! Mom would bake cookies for hours and the irresistible cookie aroma would fill the house and give you a warm and comfy feeling, but it also made you drool for more cookies. The reason Mom would make so many cookies is because she would wrap up about 10 big plates of cookies and we would all get in the car and start to make some friendly visits.

Mom would stop in to visit people she knew and worked with at their place of business, schools, doctor's office—we went all over visiting people Mom knew. It was always a hoot to watch the expressions of everyone when they saw us walking through the front door with a platter full of freshly baked cookies. Mom would introduce her three boys, me being the oldest, then Ben, and Chris the youngest. Mom would give us a quick motivational pep talk before we went into each place. "I love you boys, but if you do anything to embarrass Mommy, you will meet Jesus!"

My brothers and I were pretty hyperactive kids and liked to run in every direction and do whatever our sugar coated minds would jump to next. However, in this particular case, there were cookies involved and so we were not about to jeopardize our shot at getting more cookies from Mom. We behaved like little angels.

Mom would hand the plate over to the person she knew and they would immediately pull back the top foil covering the cookies, lower the tray to the eye level of the three perfectly behaved boys, and ask,

"Would you boys like a cookie?"

Our eyes doubled in size with excitement, but when we looked at Mom to check if it would be okay or not, she would give us the so called "MOM LOOK" which meant "NO" and to thankfully decline the offer. Each of Mom's cookie visits lasted only a few minutes and then we would be on our way to the next place.

Sometimes those cookies would be so tempting I would become hypnotized by them and actually thought about tipping the cookie plates over and telling Mom, *"I don't think these cookies are any good any more, they landed on the floor ... I guess we should eat them ... I mean throw them away."*

I never did flip the plate of cookies over, but I sure thought about it—a lot! As I write this and the craving of freshly baked cookies fills my mind, looking back I wish I had flipped a few of those plates.

Growing up, I learned that you visit people you know or do business with and properly introduce your family. Now, over 30 years later, my family was on their way over to the new accountant's office. We didn't have time to grab cookies, but we had a two-month-old and that can be just as entertaining. We arrived, walked in and they welcomed us. We exchanged pleasantries for only a few minutes and we were on our way.

A few days passed when I walked outside to grab the mail for the day. It was mostly junk mail, but there was a letter from our new accountant's office. I thought maybe they sent a letter saying, "*Sam, it was great of you to stop in and introduce your family. Your wife is amazing. Your daughter is precious. We are excited to work with you and if we can do anything for you or answer any questions, don't hesitate to call us anytime.*"

Those are the best letters to get from people you are about engage in business with. I tore open the envelope, unfolded the letter and I didn't see any of those magic words or sentiments in it. In fact, it wasn't a letter at all, it was a bill. A bill! I scrolled to the bottom of the bill where it stated a new balanced owed in the amount of $80. I was dumbfounded because we hadn't done any work yet. So I glanced at the description of the invoice and it said: *15 minute visit with client's wife and baby.*

My mouth dropped to the ground. *"Really?!! Are you kidding me? They sent us a bill for stopping in to say hello and we weren't even there for 15 minutes! Ahhh!! That is some shady stuff."*

I was more than disappointed and felt like I had just got punched in the gut by someone I really needed to rely on and trust. Later that week we bumped into the new accountant in the grocery store, he walked up to us with a big smile and greeted us with simple pleasantries. I jokingly said to him, *"We would love to talk with you right now, however we are on a fixed budget and can't afford another $80 bill to chitchat with you."*

He had a confused look on his face at first and then it sunk in. Now his face began to turn red with embarrassment and he got the picture. We would have been a great customer for his firm for years and years, but that one simple act of low class cost him our business. I am not debating whether his time is valuable or not, but there is an etiquette and integrity factor involved. If this guy charges me $80 for simple *"hellos"* and blindsides us with that kind of invoice, imagine what other things he might surprise us with if we continued working with him. It made me feel that, if I can't trust him with the little things, I definitely won't be able to trust him with the bigger and more important things. My family is the most important thing, and when you charge me $80 for a few minutes of introductions, you demonstrate that you don't respect what is truly valuable to me.

The gift of integrity is about owning the words and promises you put out there. It is communicating truthfulness. If the accountant had informed me that any office visit is an on the clock visit, I would have respected that guideline for his way of business. I might not agree with it, but I would have respected him and his organization a lot more had they communicated instead of doing something disreputable.

I recall not so long ago an experience I had with my printer, which demonstrated what integrity is genuinely all about. I was on a deadline for a conference I would be speaking at and my client ordered 400 books for everyone in the audience. I had about 150 or so left in stock, and in order to fulfill the demand, I needed to place a rush order with my printer. My printer is a great guy who is always busy and, like me, can be a little forgetful if he doesn't write something down or have it in front of him. I let him know that if the books didn't arrive by a certain date, it wouldn't work. He promised and assured me the books would be shipped out on a certain date so I would save on shipping costs. The day for shipping came and it was about 20 minutes to 5 o'clock. I hadn't received a tracking number for the shipment, so I called the printer to verify the books got mailed to the conference. He forgot. Not only did the books not ship out, he forgot to print the books.

I was a little bummed because I knew my client really wanted to give everyone a copy of my book and they even worked to get a VIP sponsor to pay for the books. I figured there was no solution and there was nothing I could do about it. I wasn't about to cancel future business with my printer, because he does great work and his service is usually top notch. Sometimes things go wrong and this was one of those moments. We just had to deal with it and move on from it. I said, "Hey man, don't worry about it. You are busy and this stuff happens. I will do better to order earlier in future so there isn't such a rush."

My printer apologized repeatedly, but at this point it was no longer a big deal to me. But it was to him! My printer is a person who is aware of his promises and owns them. He stands by the quality of his work and the integrity of his word. He went into his print shop, worked all through the night and all the next day to print and bind my books and then personally paid to overnight the books to my client. I didn't ask him to do that for me. He didn't have to do that for me. So why would he do such a thing? He has a high level of integrity.

Some people still believe in doing right by others. Integrity means something to them. He hardly made a penny on this print job, but he stayed true to his word and gave me one of the best gifts there is in this world—the gift of integrity. People who practice integrity are first class. Own what you say you will do. If you can't live up to your word then admit it, fix it if you can and do better next time.

The Gift of Positive Communication

I just came from an interesting dinner and feel like I need an antacid, a nap and possibly a priest—not because of the food, but because of all the bickering and back and forth fighting that came from the restaurant staff where I was dining. All the patrons dining could hear the ruckus of toxic communication and escalating drama. I felt like I needed to confess my sins to a priest to free myself of all the toxic and dirty communication going on around me. They were fighting about whose job it was to do this, and who didn't do that and who is to blame because of that. Then, from the back, appears what might be a restaurant manager. Apart of me thought, "Oh good, someone to put an end to this out of control rodeo show."

The manager quickly stepped into the mix of all the bickering between the employees and, instead of putting an end to the mounting drama, he jumped into it like someone who just did a cannon ball into a swimming pool. The bickering got louder and people started getting up to leave the restaurant. I should have as well, but a part of me thought it would get better—it didn't.

Trying to lighten up the atmosphere of negativity, I said in a low tone to some people sitting next to me, "Isn't this how CSI or a scene from Cops starts out?"

You just got the vibe that, at some point, there was going to be a 911 call involved and cops would have to swarm the place to restore order to what was happening. When I got up to leave, I felt sick to my stomach. That kind of behavior gives me heartburn. My expectation of a relaxing and laid back dinner was kaput. So to make myself feel better I walked over to the Dairy Queen, got the biggest ice cream cone they had and was able to decompress the stress a little. *(Believe it or not, dairy actually calms the nerves. And the sugar, well that's just fantastic!)*

Teamwork requires people who are willing to use positive communication to make things happen. It is easy to point fingers, blame, complain, ridicule and raise your voice, but it doesn't solve anything or bring people together. There may be times when your gut response is to go off on someone because they did something or didn't do something that affected others, but blowing up only fuels the disengagement. Our communication often determines the response in others. You have to have the awareness of what kind of return you want your communication to have.

Not too long ago, I got stuck in an elevator with seven other people at the O'Hare airport in Chicago. With seven people, it was crowded; it felt more like 100 people. I was tired and ready to get to the parking garage and go home. But as soon as the door closed, we went up about a foot and then the elevator just stopped.

It was quiet for a few seconds until someone spoke up, "Hey, I think we are stuck."

And I think his name may have been Sherlock because someone said to him, "No kidding, Sherlock! Yeah we are stuck!"

The woman standing next to all the buttons pushed the emergency button and, as we waited calmly for an emergency response, a voice over the intercom system filled the elevator with what could only be assumed was one angry person. The man speaking through the intercom started yelling at us, "Why did you break my elevator?! What did you do to my elevator?!!"

It is safe to say this individual obviously did not understand the gift of positive communication.

I started thinking, *how is yelling at people stuck in an elevator a good idea? It's not! It made a bad situation worse. What clues do you need to understand this?*

The yelling created panic, multiplied the stress

levels and infused the atmosphere with unnecessary fear. It made people angry and several reciprocated by yelling back, "We didn't break your @#$%& elevator! But, when I get out of here I am going to break your face with my fist!"

It got pretty ugly for a few minutes. In fact, someone even started to cry, wet themselves and tried to curl up in a ball out of pure fear. I would like to say that was not one of my finest moments in life and one I would like to forget, but I was a little stressed and scared.

Finally, another voice came on over the intercom. It was the calm voice of someone who understood positive communication, "Folks, I am sorry for the inconvenience. Please stay calm. We are fixing the elevator and will have you out of there in a jiffy."

After that, the response of everyone in the elevator was calm. Some even started cracking a few jokes. I am pretty sure someone could have benefited from some Tic Tacs, Mentos or any brand of mouth wash.

Here is the lesson: The way we communicate

The way we communicate —

—determines the response in others. There are circumstances that spur instant reactions that don't come across as positive and as a result there can be heated emotions, false assumptions and no resolve. The key is to be aware of your communication and know that, if you can control your communication in such a way, it will lead to positive outcomes.

In fact, this evening I was at a major retail store that I am sure most of you are familiar with. I needed some assistance at the jewelry counter to adjust my watch. So, I waited, waited more and continued to wait longer. Nobody was showing up to work the counter. I didn't feel like waiting until the sun went down for assistance, so I set off to find a manager and see if they might be able to deploy help to that area. I found the manager and asked if she might be able to have someone help me at the jewelry counter. Let me point something out, the way in which I made my request was super polite. However, my request seemed to be her tipping point for the day. She fired back at me, "Sir, I will call someone in a little bit, we are under staffed and everyone is busy."

Now, you and I both know that is no way to communicate or treat a customer, right?

I could tell she was trying to manage a lot of things at once and noticed her attitude was being driven by unmanaged stress. Her leadership stock was plummeting, so, I gently stepped a little closer in her direction and spoke with a pleasant kindness, "Hey, I can tell you have a lot going on and you seem a little stressed. Can I buy you a Snickers bar? The commercial says it helps you feel better. Or I can get a bag of cheesy Cheetos, which always helps me." She stopped, stared at me like I was somewhat insane and broke into a big smile and even began to laughed a little. There it was! She just needed some positive charge for her attitude. Her attitude wasn't working; mine was, so I gave her a piece of mine. I knew if I responded in kind to her attitude, it would only make things worse for her and me. I would still be waiting in the jewelry section 100 years later. However, I communicated in a way that got me the response I wanted, but also the person I wanted to work with. She grabbed a key and said, "I will take care of you."

As she was helping me, she said, "I don't know what you have, but we sure could use some of it around here."

I knew she was talking about my attitude. I told her who I was and what I do and that I have actually contacted her corporate office many, many, many times to offer my services, but they keep coming back with "We don't have any budgets for what you do."

She frowned and said, "That is too bad. They need to start working to improve attitudes around here because the negativity is spreading like a wild fire."

As a way to thank her and to recognize her for taking care of me, I went to my truck, grabbed some copies of my book and brought them into her. She was standing around a few people and you would have thought I scored a touchdown she was so excited.

Richard Branson said it best, "Mighty companies

are losing their might because they don't keep investing in quality training."

I would agree with that. When you cut the budgets that make people better it has to be an indication that negative consequences will follow. If you have people who don't deliver quality customer service, you are communicating to your customers, "We don't value you enough to make the adjustments to serve you in a way that makes you want to keep doing business with us."

As an example, the national retailer I just shared about is rated second to last in customer service next to tech support services. What they lack is accountability and consistency to their training. You can still cut costs and give customers savings, but you can also train people to be great in the process. Leaders would benefit more; profit the organization's bottom line more, if they put some attention on assisting people on becoming the best version of themselves. Because as a customer, isn't that what we really want? We wanted to be treated with someone's best.

Better communication starts with engaging leadership. The way you handle pressure communicates to others how they should handle stress and unexpected change. Whatever attitude and efforts you want to see demonstrated by others, it is up to you to communicate that example and expectation.

One significant component of communication is listening. When you listen, and I mean truly listen, it communicates that you are engaged and value what the other person is communicating. It means you are not re-loading your thoughts to respond, but are in tune and seeking to understand what is being communicated to you. When you listen, you don't miss the important stuff. It is one thing to hear what others are saying, but it's another when you listen and process the information in a way that lets others know it's not going in one ear and out the other.

Another component of communication is learning the ways people respond best. This form of communication adds personalization to the mix. It involves discovering the best ways to communicate and connect with your children, spouse, friends, or co-workers. Everyone is a little different. The same key doesn't work on every lock; it requires some effort to learn what form of communication connects with others. Some people might retain your communication better if you write it down and leave them a note. You have to be observant of what makes your communication connect best with others. You may need to schedule your communication time so nobody is left guessing, mind reading, or conjuring up false assumptions. How you communicate determines responses from others, so put the right effort into mastering your communication to connect effectively with others.

Sam Glenn

The Gift of
a Better You

A friend, who manages a successful company, shared with me his philosophy on why he buys everyone books and promotes personal improvement in the workplace.

"I want my employees to work harder on themselves than they do their job. When they get better at who they are, they become awesome at what they do."

I heard this quote once and it has stayed with me since, "When we get better, it becomes a gift to others."

If you want to be a better parent, spouse, co-worker or leader, it starts when you choose to keep improving and working on who you are.

Since I travel over a hundred some days a year, at one time my eating habits got a little out of control. I would skip breakfast and buy junk food at the gas station to keep me going on my drives. And then I would order up room service around 9pm at night and eat a large portion of fatty foods before bed. When you do this once in a while it really doesn't hurt you, but the things you do consistently begin to build and move you in certain directions.

I put on my pants one day and realized I needed a new pair. I looked in the mirror and didn't like what I was seeing. So, in order for me to feel good about myself, be healthy for my family and have healthy energy levels, I needed to make some improvements to my eating habits.

I started researching how to lose weight, but also how to eat better so I would be full longer and not have crazy cravings before I went to bed. And it is important to understand that personal improvement is a process, not a race. I needed to lose over 50lbs and eating good for one day here and there wasn't going to get the job done. I needed to alter my current habits and create new ones. As I improved, I noticed my life got better. As I got more energy, it became a gift to me and to others.

Personal improvement isn't solely about our weight or food; it can be about a number of things. It can be about eliminating a bad habit or some influence that brings out your worst. It can be about your attitude. I can't tell you how many times people have come up to me after my speech and said, "Hey, can you come talk to my boss/wife/kids/husband? They need a new attitude."

They key to a better you is making the choice to work on what needs working on. But, here is the deal. When you work on a better you it also becomes professional improvement. Like my friend said, when we become better at who we are, we become awesome at what we do. We care more, do more, and give our best.

Here is my **10 Step Attitude Maintenance Plan** to get you thinking more positively and feeling more energized. It is a very simple list and you can easily do this.

1. Create a personal self improvement plan.

What do you need to change about you?

What weakness keeps tripping you up that you need to work on?

How much time are you willing to dedicate to working on yourself—a week, a day?

Like the saying goes, "What gets measured gets improved."

You need to develop some personal goals for your personal development journey.

Do you need to learn how to be better with your money?

Do you need to learn to cook better meals?

Do you have issues with time management? An addiction?

Do it the old fashioned way and get a pen and

notepad out and start to write down the following:

    a. What you want to work on.

    b. What you can do to work on it.

    c. Then do it!

2. **Research your topic as it relates to your improvement plan and goals.** Research what you want to get better at. YouTube offers a lot of videos that can assist you with your topic of choice. There are numerous articles written on just about every subject there is. Before we had our daughter, I researched How to Be a Good Dad. I found a lot of great ideas and started to put them into action.

3. **Inventory your influences.** What or who do you allow to influence your life? Creating an inventory of your influences means asking the questions, "Is this good for me? Does it bring out the best in me—or the worst?" What you permit is what you promote—so determine what needs boundaries, or more access. What you let influence your life will contribute to the face of

your attitude. If you go grab a drink with the guys after work just about every other night, and it translates into less time with your family which is affecting your relationships, then you need to change some influences. Go out less. If watching TV before you go to bed is keeping you up longer, change the influence and do something else that will allow you to get better sleep. I used to fall asleep on the couch every night and wake up hours later with all sorts of back pain. Instead of falling asleep on the couch, I needed to change the situation by changing my action. If you like beer and it shows up in the form of a big belly, it means you need to change something. Same goes with smoking or any other habit that isn't working for you. Change your influence and you will change your outcomes.

4. **Move, move, move**. This philosophy is "Don't take the elevator; take the stairs." The fastest way to feel better about yourself and life is to move your body. There is no way you are going to lose

that 5, 10, or 25 pounds by sitting on the couch and eating junk food late at night. You don't need a magic pill to lose fat; you just need a plan, and to move. Food is energy for the human body. Develop a new perspective about food so you don't overeat—but rather you have some food management skills. Buy a healthy cookbook and learn to cook. Let me say it in a nice way, "Just get off your butt and do something!" If you are overweight, unhappy, and that statement offends you, maybe it will offend you enough to do something about it. Trust me; I used to be very unhealthy until I got offended—not by what anyone said, but by looking in the mirror. I didn't like what I saw, so I got offended and did something about it. Getting offended is sometimes the best motivation to change for the better.

5. **Make a list of thoughts you want to become the most <u>dominant</u> in your mind.** See yourself achieving a goal. Play that mental picture over and over again in your mind. Play it in such

a way that you feel like it has happened. Before I became an author, I pictured myself signing thousands of autographs. I pictured and practiced so much in my mind that, years later, when I became an author, I would do book signings for up to three and four hours non-stop. People would continue to ask me if I was getting tired. I would answer, "No way, I have been practicing for this a long time—years in fact!"

Thing of things you want to do, become, achieve. The goal is to focus on what you want to move towards. So many times we focus on our weaknesses that we stay partnered with defeating and doubtful thoughts. It's time to change that style ofthinking and focus to something that rewards you.

6. **Have a good diet plan.** Develop a better food plan than flying through the fast food place on a whim. Move to eating salads, raw nuts, and vegetables. Remember, food is fuel for the

body. Manage your food in such a way that it energizes you.

7. **Have good accountability so you don't slip up or give up**. You can't expect to achieve the results you want if you expect others to do the work for you or if you make up excuses as to why you can't make your improvement happen. Setting up some accountability is informing someone you trust or has your best interests at hand and asking them to hold you to your mission. For example, I started asking my brother to work out with me. We worked out for about 2 weeks straight and then I started thinking of excuses not to work out so I could rest or do something else. He would not let me out of my agreement, so I had to go. This is the one reason why New Year's resolutions go flop, they lack accountability. We all start off strong in the pursuit of our goals to improve, but after a while we kind of start to slip—little by little. And soon it begins to add up. And then we start to justify our behavior, "Well, if

I don't work out today, I will eat less tomorrow and work out for an extra hour." It sounds good, until the next day arrives and we don't follow through. Accountability is having someone who will not accept your excuses and won't let you out of your agreement to achieve your goals. And sometimes they aren't always nice when we begin to resist and stray from our goal. My brother would come to my house and get me, or call my wife and tattle on me that I wasn't following through—he made it very difficult to bail on following through. Accountability is a huge key to ensuring you follow through on your game plan.

8. Rest up to recharge up. Make sure you get enough rest so your body is efficiently recharged with energy. Depriving yourself of rest will hurt your body and mental state. Get enough sleep. Studies show that lack of sleep will affect your attitude, performance, and health, and cause you to gain extra weight.

9. **Feed your attitude.** Feed your attitude positive information. This book is food for your attitude. Your attitude becomes and grows into whatever you feed it. Your attitude is something that is always at work—working for you or against you, you determine which. What you feed your mind will be input and then output in your work, relationships, and life. If you don't like your behavior (your output), then you need to begin to change your input. Begin to read good material; listen to positive words and music.

Personally, I love positive quotes. They are fast and easy to read and are like a vitamin for your attitude.

10. Surround yourself with healthy thinking people. I like what a friend told me once, "We need to spend more time with those who celebrate us than those who simply tolerate us."

This means you have to let go of some of the 'toxic people' in your life or create boundaries with them. Often we want to change others or situations, but the key is in knowing that we can't ... but we can change ourselves and our attitude by how we deal with others and situations.

Nothing is worth getting into a mud fight over with someone negative. It's like wrestling with a pig. The only difference is you both get muddy and the pig likes it. (Think about that one for a minute.)

As much as we want negative people to stop being so negative, it is not up to us to change them. That is not our responsibility. The only person you can change is YOU. If you want to influence a negative person to join the positive side, you can set an example. You can lead others to the water, but it will be up to them to drink.

The Gift of

Love

It is said that, when we look back on our lives, we will think one of two things, *"I am glad I did," or "I wish I had."*

I found an interesting story in the newspaper that shared a moving story about love. The location of the story was somewhere in Florida. Now, you know in Florida they often deal with alligator problems. A young boy was out playing near a retention pond while his mom washed dishes and watched him through the kitchen window. Suddenly, an alligator jumped out of the water and grabbed onto the boy's leg. The mom ran to the boy in a frantic state of panic and began the tug of war for her son. She was pulling him so hard her fingernails dug into the boy's arms. As others came to their aid, the alligator let go of the boy's leg. They quickly rushed the boy to the hospital and the doctors were able to save his leg.

Years later, the local press did a story on that boy, now a young man. They asked him questions about his escape from the alligator and took pictures of the bite scar on his leg, but he wanted to tell the press about some other scars he got that day. He rolled up his sleeves and showed them the scars on his arms from his mother's fingernails. He told them that he was thankful for those scars. "Every day when I look at these scars, I am grateful because these are scars of love – the love my Mom had for me the day she would not let go of me and fought for my life against the alligator."

Is there someone you have wanted to spend time with but things have just gotten away from you? I recall hearing a story about a little boy named Jonny.

His mother had cancer and a very short time left to live. One day, the town minister came to pay a visit and check up on the mother. They spent some time talking, when the mother made a special request of the minister, "Would you be willing to explain to Jonny what is happening to me and what will happen so he understands?"

The minister agreed, and found Jonny playing outside in their yard. He asked the boy to sit next to him on the backdoor steps. He knew Jonny was young and may not understand all of what he was going to explain, but he did his best. He explained to Jonny how his mom was sick and that he should spend as much time with her as possible while she was still there. Jonny asked the minister how much time he had with his mommy. The minister thought for a moment, pointed over to the big tree in their backyard, and said, "When the leaves begin to fall from that big tree that is when your mommy will be leaving you. So while she is still here, you need to spend as much time with her as you can."

Jonny nodded his head to convey he understood the minister's message. Weeks went by and the season of fall was nearing. The air became cooler, the color of the leaves began to change and the days became shorter. The minister wanted to check in on Jonny's sick mother, so one afternoon he made his way to their house for a little visit.

He pulled up a chair and sat next to the mother, who was resting on the couch and appeared weaker than she had during his previous visit. He held her hand to show support and care, "So, have you been able to spend some quality time with Jonny?"

She shook her head. "Not as much as I would like. He is always in the backyard."

"Really? Let me go out back and say hi to Jonny and see how he is doing."

The minister walked out the back door, but Jonny was not in sight. "Jonny!? Jonny!? Where are you?"

The little boy startled the minister by shouting down from up in the big tree, "Hey—I am up here!"

Looking up, the minister saw Jonny in the big tree

with a huge brown bag filled with leaves and a big roll of tape. He was taping all the fallen leaves back onto the tree.

"Jonny, what are you doing?"

Sadly, the young boy explained his efforts in one sentence, "I am taping leaves back on the tree because I don't want my mommy to go away."

That story may tug on your heart a little, it did mine. But the reason I shared it was to give a moving example that we have to make the most of the precious and limited time we have with others. We have to make it count. The gifts we give through our attitude spell out love. It is not so much about how you love or when, but how much others feel your love. Sometimes we get so busy we neglect what matters most. Have you ever done that? A story like Jonny's is a wakeup call to seize the day and use the gifts you have to make someone feel loved.

Sometimes, love shows up in the most unique ways.

One thing I do with my wife is ask her, "What can

I do to make you feel more loved today?" For her it is just a few brief minutes of my attention and some hugs. It doesn't seem much to me, but to her it is everything that love is.

Love can be demonstrated in so many ways—words, gifts, time, actions and touch. It can be sitting with someone and just listening. Your presence can be an act of love. You don't need to have solutions for them; just being there is what makes them feel loved. Love can be admitting you were wrong about something and owning the situation. Love may be watching what someone else wants to watch on TV because you know it is their favorite show, even though you can't stand it. The demonstration of love is a wonderful gift. Don't hold it in, rather step out of your comfort zone, make the time, and do something that demonstrates one of the greatest gifts we can give to each other—LOVE!

The Gift of

Hope

Sometimes, having a little hope that whatever is going on in life will work out for the best and that everything will be okay is the most comforting gift in the world. A little hope is like a nightlight that shines in the dark. Hope gives us something to look forward to. Hope gives us strength to hold on through the storms of life. Hope chases away our fears and anxieties. A little hope can go a long way. Hope gives us a clear view of all we have to be thankful for. There have been moments in my own life when having a little hope was like getting some fresh air. I felt like I could breathe and like heavy weights had been lifted off my chest. Hope is such a powerful gift.

The following story is one of my all-time favorites. It gives me hope to keep looking forward in positive ways. I hope you like it as well.

Emma was in her 80s and was given news from her doctor that she was terminally ill and didn't have much time left. She invited her pastor over to go over her funeral arrangements for when the time came. As they sat at the kitchen table, Emma laid out her requests. "Pastor, when I am lying in the casket, and people come to pay their respects, I would like in my right hand the Bible. And in my left hand I would like you to place a fork."

Puzzled by the fork request, the pastor inquired as to why.

"Since I was a little girl, I have been to pot luck dinners, fundraisers and elegant dinners. After the main course, when the wait staff would remove the dishes, they'd always tell you to hang onto your fork. I

always smiled because I knew it meant the best was yet to come—dessert. And so as I lay there I want people to see that fork and know that no matter what's going on in their life, the best is yet to come."

Sometimes just a little hope fills our heart in such a way that, no matter what is going on, we know everything will work out in a good way. Hope is one of the best gifts we can give others. One story that stays with me comes from when I was waiting to board a flight in Indianapolis. There was a young man sitting across from me who was also waiting for the same flight. He looked broken and scared. He leaned over to the older gentleman sitting next to him and almost started to cry. "Excuse me, sir. I hate to bother you. I am so tired. I am a recovering addict and trying to get home. I need to close my eyes for a few minutes and I don't want to fall asleep and miss this flight. Will you wake me up when we board?"

The gentleman agreed. It was as if that gentleman was assigned to be this young man's guardian angel. He continued to sip his coffee and read the paper, but was alert to this young man and his well-being. When the boarding started, he calmly woke the young man and I could not hear what the words being exchanged were, but the young man nodded in agreement as the older gentleman spoke to him. You could tell that whatever he was sharing was helping this young man. Perhaps the young man zeroed out in life and had hit rock bottom, maybe people had given up on him and maybe he was close to giving up on himself, but the words of the older gentleman filled this young man with some life. It was like night and day. The boy no longer looked so scared or jittery. It was as if the words were calming him and helping him to see that, despite everything going on, there was hope. From my point of view it was a selfless act of love that filled someone's attitude tank with exactly what it was deficient of—HOPE!

And Now,

It's Up To You...

In closing, I will say it one last time, "Your attitude is either in the way or making a way and you determine which every day."

I have highlighted the most inspiring ways to create exceptional experiences for others. It's up to how you use your attitude every day. You can use it to hurt or heal, encourage or discourage, give or take. It is up to you. The key point to remember is that making a difference doesn't have to be complicated; using your attitude to make someone feel special is simple and can be enjoyable. You just have to be aware of your attitude and look for opportunities to use it to make situations better. We can give the gift of attitude to anyone and the impact it may have might vary, but ultimately it is wrapped in love and meaningful to others.

Choose the way of the Attitude Warrior. If someone's attitude isn't working right, instead of getting upset and defensive, choose to give them a little bit of your attitude. Put your attitude at the top of your priority list at work and in life, and you will begin to see what a wonderful gift it really is. I hope you enjoyed this book and if you know anyone who might benefit from it, please share your copy with them or get them one as a gift.

There are probably other ideas on how to spread the gift of attitude or maybe you have a personal story and want to share. I love reading them. Sometimes they end up in a future book or a speech because they are so awesome (names excluded of course). Feel free to email if you would like to share: Sam@SamGlenn.com

About Sam Glenn

The Attitude Guy ©

With Sam Glenn, *"It's all about attitude!"* Sam went from working nights as a janitor – negative, depressed, uptight and sleeping on the floor – to discovering his calling, happiness, humor and a king size Serta mattress. They say the two most memorable moments of any event are the opening and the closing. Sam Glenn is widely known as one of the most entertaining and energizing speakers to kick off conferences and wrap them up. At one time, Sam's most terrifying fear was public speaking; years later, he has won multiple awards for his speeches, been named Speaker of the Year by several organizations and spoken to audiences as large as

75,000 people at stadium events. Today, Sam delivers close to 100 uplifting speeches a year to organizations and conference events that focus on recharging people's attitude batteries. As Sam humorously likes to share, *"I don't use PowerPoint in my presentations. I don't need it. I have ADHD, which means ---I am the PowerPoint!"*

Sam and his family currently reside in Carmel, Indiana, but are originally from Stillwater Minnesota. In his free time, he likes to fish, collect funny stories and practice anger management skills on the golf course. Sam is always grateful for word of mouth, so if you enjoyed this book and know someone who might benefit from it, please spread some attitude by telling others.

To inquire about speaking engagements, email Sam's office: **contact@samglenn.com**

Visit the Official Website for Sam Glenn:

www.SamGlenn.com